HOPS AND DREAMS

HOPS AND DREAMS

The Story of Sierra Nevada Brewing Co.

Rob Burton

STANSBURY
PUBLISHING
Chico, Ca.

HOPS AND DREAMS
The Story of Sierra Nevada Brewing Co.
Copyright © 2010 by Rob Burton
First Edition
Printed in the United States of America

ISBN 978-1-935807-01-8 paperback
ISBN 978-1-935807-02-5 hardcover

Noncredited photos courtesy of Sierra Nevada Brewing Co.

Stansbury Publishing
An Imprint of Heidelberg Graphics
2 Stansbury Court
Chico, California 95928

Library of Congress Cataloging-in-Publication Data

Burton, Robert Stacey, 1955-
  Hops and dreams : the story of Sierra Nevada Brewing Co. / Rob Burton. -- 1st ed.
    p. cm.
  Includes bibliographical references and index.
  Summary: "On November 15, 1980, two young homebrewers opened a microbrewery in northern California. Thirty years later, Sierra Nevada Brewing Co. is widely recognized as a leader of the craft brewing revolution. This is the story of the company's rise to success"-- Provided by publisher.
  ISBN 978-1-935807-01-8 (pbk.) -- ISBN 978-1-935807-02-5 (hardcover)
  1. Sierra Nevada Brewing Co. 2. Brewing industry--California--Chico. 3. Microbreweries--California--Chico. I. Title.
  HD9397.U54S543 2010
  338.7'663420979432--dc22

                                                                    2010040015

"I drink to the general joy of the whole table."

—William Shakespeare

CONTENTS

CHAPTER FOUR
In Pursuit of Hop Harmony
2000–2010

CHAPTER FIVE
Hop Harmony at Work: Sierra Nevada and the Triple P
(People, Planet, Profit)

CONCLUSION

APPENDIX

GLOSSARY OF TERMS

WORKS CITED

INDEX

ACKNOWLEDGMENTS

WITHOUT THE genius and entrepreneurial daring of Ken Grossman and Paul Camusi, this book would not exist. I am grateful to them for turning their dream into a reality, one that could be enjoyed by so many. In particular, I would like to thank Ken Grossman who was consistently patient, courteous, and thorough in answering my questions about his company and the brewing industry generally. Thanks also to the members of Ken's family who provided valuable feedback: Eleanor (his mother), Katie (his wife), Steve (his elder brother), Sierra and Brian (his children).

I wish I could use this space to acknowledge everyone associated with Sierra Nevada Brewing Co.—past, present, and future. That would be impossible, of course. Nevertheless, I thank those of you who unfailingly responded to my e-mail inquiries and who were always available for on-site interviews. In alphabetical order, they are: Carrie Alden, Bill Bales, Cheri Chastain, Marie Gray, Laura Harter, Scott Jennings, Alan Judge, Bill Manley, Jim Mellem, and Gil Sanchez. (Laura Harter and Bill Manley deserve a special mention: Laura for helping to coordinate my interviews, Bill for providing me with photographs and for the lively Taproom chats). In addition, the following people took time out of their busy schedules to meet with me (often more than once) thus helping to educate me about the world of beer: Steve Dresler, Rob Fraser, Micheal Iles, Charles Kyle, Bob Littell, and Terence Sullivan. To the front-desk receptionists who greeted me with a friendly smile and to the bartenders, waiters, and waitresses who went about their business with grace and charm, I salute your consummate professionalism.

My thanks to two Chico-based architects, Ed Hoiland and Matt Gallaway, who took time to describe in detail their blueprints for the brewery. Also, to Fritz Pfister, an engineer at Huppmann, the German company from whom Sierra Nevada purchased its elegant brewing kettles.

Professor Michael Lewis, a connoisseur of brewing science, was gracious enough to meet me in Davis to share his wealth of knowledge about the brewing industry in general and Sierra Nevada's significance in particular.

This book started out as a team project. Lee Altier, Andy Flescher, Steve Metzger, and Bob Speer helped to shape the book; Steve and Bob also offered worthy suggestions on how to craft the story in its early stages. In addition, Vern Andrews, Charlie Geshekter, Bruce Grelle, and Bill Paris were diligent readers of various draft versions; their feedback was always greatly appreciated.

Mark Gailey constantly supplied me with snippets of information relevant to the book, for which I am most grateful.

It was a privilege to work with Larry Jackson, my publisher. I truly appreciate his dedication and diligence, not to mention his subtle sense of humor which would always surface at exactly the appropriate moment.

Thanks to Leili and Sofie for putting up with my beer talk for three years, and for consistently encouraging me to persist with the project.

Finally, I would like to express my thanks to the craft brewing community in general: I have learned much from reading your blogs, attending your conferences, subscribing to your trade journals, and drinking your beer. And I've come to the conclusion that worthy values such as "passion" and "dedication" are part of your DNA.

I apologize for any mistakes or misrepresentations that may appear in the book. They are entirely my responsibility.

INTRODUCTION

WHY WRITE a book about beer? I've been asked this question often. In fact, I sometimes ask it of myself. After all, I'm not directly involved in the brewing business. Sure, I enjoy the taste of beer, particularly its bitter, hoppy flavors. However, I confess that I don't understand the intricate science of beer's production. If you asked me the meaning of the word "flocculation" before I started this book, I would have said it was either a farming ritual to herd sheep or some type of ancient torture technique. The truth is I'm a college English professor who is more used to measuring syllables in a poem than counting hop bitterness units in a beer. My one and only experiment with homebrewing ended in disaster when untamed yeast foamed wildly out of a white bucket onto the wood floor of my student apartment leaving a stain and a stench that resulted in the loss of my security deposit.

So why would I want to write a book about beer? As is often the case with such "big" questions, there is both a short and long answer.

Here's the short answer. When I moved to northern California in August 1988, to assume a teaching position at California State University, Chico, I quickly became aware of a local microbrewery with a fiercely loyal following. Its distinctive beer was readily available in the supermarkets, at faculty dinner parties, even at the annual campus reception. This brewery, as colleagues, students, and strangers would point out with pride, was Sierra Nevada Brewing Co. Its flagship Pale Ale had, by the late '80s, attracted national attention yielding profits that allowed its co-owners, Ken Grossman and Paul Camusi, to move from a converted warehouse (where they had been brewing since 1980) into a state-of-the-art 100-barrel brew house that opened with a flourish in 1988, just a few months prior to my arrival in Chico.

Over the years, I watched it grow into the sixth largest brewery in the United States and emerge as one of the nation's most successful and influential craft breweries. In a sense, I feel that I have grown up with it over the past two decades. I have regularly enjoyed its beers in the company of family and friends at the brewery's Taproom and Restaurant and at home during a ritual happy hour in the afternoon when I settle down with a good book and a pleasing brew after a day of teaching. Often, in the early morning as I ride my bike to the college campus through Lower Bidwell Park, the rich porridge smell from roasting barley malt in the brewery two miles away mixes with the sharp scent of pine and eucalyptus, and I ask myself, "Can Paradise be far away?" (In actual fact, it is ten miles up the hill from Chico; the town of Paradise, that is).

By telling the story of Sierra Nevada Brewing Co., I wanted to share with readers some of the pleasure that I have experienced over the years. I thought I could also learn one or two things about brewing science—in particular, why my single experiment with homebrewing resulted in the production of overzealous cappuccino-like foam rather than amber-colored, liquid alcohol.

But such a relatively short answer does not quite get to the heart of the matter. In order to reveal the deeper reason for writing this book, I feel I need to reach further into my personal background, thus spinning a tale best told over a few drinks perhaps. I'll need to start with some basics: my name and birthplace. And so here's the long answer for which I beg your indulgence.

I am a Burton who hails from the southeast county of Kent in England.

That may seem innocent enough at first. But behind these two facts are important revelations about beer and what might draw me to write about it.

To beer historians, the name Burton has a special significance. In Victorian England, the town of Burton-on-Trent, situated in the industrial Midlands, came to be associated with a relatively new beer style—the pale ale. Up until that time, Britain's beer of choice had been the porter with its dark, malty, robust profile, particularly popular with the dockworkers of London. But in the 1830s, it was discovered that the hard waters of Burton, rich in magnesium and calcium sulphate, enhanced hop flavors—lending beer a drier, bitterer flavor, and a brighter appearance. The pale ale was born, soon to be followed by its cousin, the India pale ale—with an even stronger hop profile. "Bitters," as they came to be called, continued to win over the drinking public. By the mid-1880s, there were thirty-one breweries in Burton, producing over three million barrels of beer a year. The town's most successful brewery, Bass, had become the biggest brewing company in the world. To this day, Bass Ale—known by its trademark red triangle—is a bottled beer you'll find prominently displayed in the beer import section of most U.S. supermarkets.

(Ironically, yet tellingly, Bass is now owned by the multinational conglomerate, Anheuser-Busch InBev. In 2008, the Belgian-Brazilian brewing company, InBev, merged with Anheuser-Busch to create the largest beer company in the world, and proceeded to gobble up smaller companies like Bass. Along with the other beer behemoth SAB Miller-Coors, they account for over 75 percent of the U.S. beer market).

I am not sure whether my ancestral lineage stretches back to the town of Burton. But I like to think that a particular kind of serendipity is at work here. Surely, it's no coincidence that I inherited a name synonymous with hoppy, bitter beers—my favorite style. Or that I am one of the rare people to enjoy the taste of Marmite—a thick paste extracted from brewer's yeast, often used as a sandwich spread, and made famous by Burton's Bass Brewery. Or that I would spend most of my adult life in Chico,

California, a town that resurrected the popularity of the pale ale by lending it a distinctive American profile.

Another thread needs unraveling. I was born in Kent, England, a fertile farming area famous for Goldings and Fuggles hops (names that conjure up musty, eccentric characters from a Dickens novel). I attended the University of Kent at Canterbury whose campus was perched on top of a hill overlooking the city dominated by the cathedral in the city center. I played cricket for the university on fields abutting hop fields. Our cricket pavilion (where we took tea and cucumber sandwiches between innings) was a converted oast house with twin conical towers that, for decades, had been used for drying hops and continued to give off a pungent, fruity smell in its locker rooms. On weekend evenings, my student friends and I would socialize at a pub called The Bishop's Finger, just beyond the East Gate of Canterbury. According to local legend, pilgrims on their way to see Thomas Beckett's shrine in the cathedral would rest here before entering through the gate into the city center. The bishop's finger, apparently, had successfully pointed them along the pilgrim's path towards the sacred shrine. When you drank in this pub, you not only slaked your thirst, you were connecting with the rhythm of history and its passing seasons. The place seemed haunted by literary characters notorious for enjoying a tipple or two: Shakespeare's Falstaff, Dickens' Mr. Pickwick, Chaucer's Wife of Bath. Fueled by pints of hand-pulled bitter, my student friends and I tried to honor their presence in our besotted discussions of James Joyce, Jack Kerouac, and the whiteness of Herman Melville's whale.

This was the mid-1970s and a revolution was taking place in England spearheaded by consumers and connoisseurs of beer, one that was about to sweep across the Atlantic on similar winds that would take me to Indiana University on a student fellowship. The revolution was called CAMRA—the Campaign for Real Ale and it called for a return to cask-conditioned beer poured by gravity rather than artificial carbonation, the kind of authentic beer

made famous by Burton breweries a century earlier. "Out with
Watney's Red Barrel, In with real ale," was the rallying cry. And
it was heard by pubs across the land. That is why on my last night
before departing to the American Midwest for graduate school, I
was to be found drinking a few pints of Shepherd Neame Kentish
Strong Ale in The Bishop's Finger pub, talking with friends about
our future destinies.

"You'd better enjoy your last drop of decent beer, Rob," my
friend Tony sympathized. "It's all piss and vinegar on the other
side of the pond, you know. You'll miss the taste of good ale once
you get over to the States."

That was August 1977, and for the next decade Tony's pre-
diction was by and large true. I spent seven of these years in the
American heartland, earning a PhD in British and American literature, and adapting to the
American palate of cold,
sugary beers which I found
to be thirst-quenching in
their way but lacking in
true bite and character. To
compensate, I would oc-
casionally indulge in an
expensive import when I
wanted to be reminded of
a beer that had something
approaching authentic flavor and body.

Then I moved to Chico
where, from the beginning,
I sensed something special
about the town—its mix
of hippy, punk, and urbane
subcultures all coming together in a deeply rural

The Bishop's Finger, Canterbury, England—where
the fresh-hopped taste of Shepherd Neame Kentish
Strong Ale still inspires bold dreams and unpredictable adventures. Courtesy of Shepherd Neame.

setting. But more impressive was its fledgling brewery. Looking back, I probably came full circle at that moment. For another revolution had taken place—one that witnessed the beer initiative passing to America, led by a group of aficionados engaged in bold brewing experiments carried out according to time-honored traditions.

Sierra Nevada's Ken Grossman and Paul Camusi were not the only pioneers in this revolution. Other important characters in the larger story of beer's renaissance in the U.S. included artisans like Fritz Maytag (Anchor Brewing Company), Jack McAuliffe (New Albion Brewing Company), Bert Grant (Yakima Brewing Company), Tom DeBakker (DeBakker Brewing Company), David Hummer and Stick Ware (Boulder Brewing Company), Chuck Coury (Cartwright Brewing Company), Paul Shipman (Redhook Ale Brewery), and on the East Coast, Jim Koch (Boston Beer Company). They were known as micro—later craft—brewers, for they signaled a return to small-scale brewing with an emphasis on taste and quality.

Most of them started out at home using a basement or garage as their workplace and cobbling equipment from local dairy farms. Yet within a decade, they had fundamentally transformed the U.S. beer industry and demonstrated that great beer could be found outside Europe—just as, a generation or two earlier, California vintners had proved that quality wines rivaling those of France and Italy could be produced domestically.

As I write this, the craft beer segment in the U.S. continues to outperform the "big beer" companies such as Anheuser-Busch InBev and SAB Miller Coors in terms of growth in domestic sales and volume production. According to the Brewers Association, an advocacy organization for the brewing industry, craft brewers (defined as "a small, independent and traditional brewer with an annual production of less than 2 million barrels") sold an estimated 8.6 million barrels of beer in 2008 and their numbers are holding steady for 2009. While it's true that "big beer" companies (those that produce over 2 million barrels of beer a year) still dominate the industry with 95 percent of overall sales in the U.S., they experienced significant sales declines for 2008 and 2009 (close to double digit declines for some brands such as Bud Light).

The craft beer revolution had been simmering well before my arrival in Chico. It was on November 15, 1980, when Grossman and Camusi brewed their first batch of stout ale—and subsequently poured it down the drain. It would take another ten batches, and several agonizing months, before they established the consistency deemed necessary for a quality beer ready to go onto the market. That year, 1980, is recognized as the founding year of Sierra Nevada Brewing Co.

Years later, in order to deepen my appreciation for this beer and the people who created it, I decided to research the history of Sierra Nevada Brewing Co. and then share the story to coincide with the company's thirtieth anniversary celebrations. The book begins with an examination of how Sierra Nevada's history intersects with the larger story of beer in an international and specifically American context. The heart of the book (chapters 2, 3, and 4) starts with Ken Grossman's arrival in Chico in 1972 and then works its way chronologically through the company's growing success and steady expansion, culminating with a series of collaboration beers released for its thirtieth anniversary celebrations. Towards the end of the book, I examine what lessons can be learned from the company's bottom-line principles, in particular its adherence to the "Triple P" mantra (People, Profit, Planet). Interwoven throughout are various vignette scenes from the Taproom bar (or "the pub," as it's known locally) over the course of the three years I was working on the book. These scenes represent the "hands-on" or participatory part of my research!

The book goes behind the scenes to tell the full story of what lies between the Taproom and the Big Room, east and west bookends of the brewery. It explores the in-between space where the actual brewing work is done. It's a compelling story of two twentysomethings from Los Angeles, Ken Grossman and Paul Camusi, who built a microbrewery in the Sierra Nevada foothills in the early 1980s—in a town whose founding-father, John Bidwell, once ran for U.S. president on the Prohibition ticket. In the course of the next twenty years, Sierra Nevada turned its flagship brew, Pale Ale, into the number one craft beer in the country, changing the tastes of a generation of beer drinkers who had grown up with sugary, carbonated, bland lagers. During that time, the company weathered the microbrewery crash of the 1990s and held out against a possible corporate takeover.

The company soon acquired a national reputation for its cutting-edge conservation policies: recycling more than 99 percent of its production waste and byproducts and reusing spent yeast, hops, grain, carbon dioxide, wastewater, and heat. Despite the cost of these policies, neither the profitability of the company nor the quality of its products was compromised. Sierra Nevada beers continue to win top honors at international beer festivals. British-born Michael Jackson, one of the world's leading authorities on craft brewing, dubbed Sierra Nevada "the Chateau Latour of American breweries" (a reference to the French vineyard famous for the high quality of its grape varieties). Additionally, much of the brewery's profits are recycled into innovative energy-saving facilities, outreach programs and local and regional nonprofit organizations—including public radio and campus cultural events.

But the story is not without its disappointments and tragedies. It is also part of a larger story that takes into account alcohol's impact on the health of individuals and society. Prohibition lasted for thirteen years in the U.S. after all, and its legacy still lives on today in prominent ways.

Surprisingly, the story has not been told before in book-length form. In fact, the brewing industry receives markedly less attention from book publishers as compared to the wine and food industries. Perhaps this is because of the unflattering stigma that surrounds beer, particularly beer drinkers who are somehow still regarded as less refined than those who partake of the grape. Or perhaps the publishing world is yet to be convinced that the twenty-first century belongs to the American craft brewer, as more and more pundits are suggesting.

Despite this lacuna, several noteworthy beer books have helped me write this book, and I wish to express my appreciation for them here. Peter Krebs' *Redhook: Beer Pioneer* (1998), Dan Baum's *Citizen Coors: An American Dynasty* (2000), and Mark Noon's *Yuengling: A History of America's Oldest Brewery* (2005), all served as useful models for me, telling the story of breweries with distinctly different profiles and trajectories. Maureen Ogle's excellent history *Ambitious Brew: The Story of American Beer* (2006) provided me with a comprehensive, chronological survey of U.S. breweries—large and small—from the mid-nineteenth century onwards. Then there are three seminal books about homebrewing, written in the 1970s and early '80s, that inspired many craft brewers (Ken Grossman included) to embark on their beer-making adventures: Fred Eckhardt's *A Treatise on Lager Beers* (1970), Byron Burch's *Quality Brewing* (1974), and Charlie Papazian's *The Complete Joy of Homebrewing* (1984). I should also like to acknowledge the late British beer connoisseur, Michael Jackson, whose many books, especially *Beer Companion* (1993), still offer the best introduction to the world of beer styles.

If my book is as interesting and flavorful to read as Sierra Nevada beer is to drink, I will feel honored and gratified. As will become evident as you read on, I agree with a quote commonly attributed to Benjamin Franklin: "Beer is living proof that God loves us and wants us to be happy." Whether or not Franklin actually used the word "beer" is still in dispute (it's more likely that he was referring to the transformative effect of rainwater on vineyards); nevertheless, as a signatory of the Declaration of Independence and the U.S. Constitution, he helped to ensure that happiness be enshrined as a cornerstone in the nation's political and cultural life. "The Constitution only gives people the right to pursue happiness. You have to catch it yourself," he proclaimed.

This book is intended to grant the reader permission to indulge happily and healthily in the story—as well as the beer—of Sierra Nevada Brewing Co., with a nod of approval from a distinguished Founding Father.

Sierra Nevada Brewing Co: where tradition meets innovation and where big dreams meet with high hopes

CHAPTER ONE

Beer History 101 and Sierra Nevada Brewing Co.

"THE MOST PERFECT BREWERY ON THE PLANET"

W HEN MICHAEL J. Lewis talks about beer, people listen. As professor emeritus at the University of California, Davis, he is recognized for establishing a program in brewing science widely regarded as the best in the nation. The book he coauthored, *Brewing,* is still rated as a flagship reference text for specialists in the brewing industry. He is a senior member of the International Brewers Guild and an elected fellow of the Institute of Brewing in London. His opinions on all beer-related matters, from wort clarification to packaging, are backed up with considerable authority and expertise. So when, halfway through a lunchtime conversation with me at Sudwerk Restaurant and Brewery in Davis, he salutes Sierra Nevada by calling it the most perfect brewery on the planet, I lower my pint of pilsner, pick up a pen, and ask if he wouldn't mind repeating himself.

"*Sierra Nevada Brewing Company is the most perfect brewery on the planet,*" he enunciates carefully. There is a glint in his eye, and I catch a faint trace of a Welsh accent as if his ancestral ways are resurfacing after four decades of living and working in the United

States. He is clearly passionate about this topic and adamant about the accuracy of his judgment.

I made the ninety-mile drive from Chico to Davis, past rice fields and almond orchards, to interview—and learn from—the man who has been at the center of a national brewing education program for more than forty years. Brewers come to Davis from all over the world to get a degree, certificate, or diploma in brewing science and technology offered at the university and its extension program. Many come specifically to work with Lewis at Sudwerk which boasts two small brewing facilities with a combined output capacity of eighty barrels. In fact, in the late 1970s, two home brewers from Chico—Ken Grossman and Paul Camusi—also came to Lewis on several occasions seeking advice about their start-up brewing business.

It's a hot mid-May afternoon; he and I are taking lunch in the shade of an expansive outdoor patio. In his forty years at the university, Lewis has taught at all levels of the brewing program—science, technology, quality control, distribution. He has trained hundreds, possibly thousands, who have gone on to become master brewers and technicians as well as brewery owners and educators.

Why would Michael Lewis make such a pronouncement about Sierra Nevada without pause or hesitation? Why would he offer the ultimate accolade to a craft brewery? After all, he is responsible to the entire brewing industry and roughly 95 percent of the U.S. market share is dominated by the big industrial brewers. A pragmatist, Michael Lewis recognizes this; the majority of his students will work for industrial breweries, not craft breweries. He is circumspect when he talks about the brewing business and avoids the binary trap that I—like many other laymen—so often succumb to, namely that craft brew is great because it's local and artisan whereas industrial brew is awful because it's national and nondescript. To confirm the point, he explains that Anheuser-Busch deserves credit and praise for mass-producing a drink that is remarkably consistent in taste. Budweiser is the perfect session beer, he declares.

"What's a session beer?" I politely ask.

"The kind of beer you drink a lot of on a hot afternoon without losing control of your faculties," he answers quickly, as if it's the standard definition he gives to his students on a routine basis. "It's not too strong, and the flavor invites you to keep going."

There seems to be a curious contradiction here. Why would he single out Sierra Nevada as the *number one* rated brewery in the world rather than, say, one of Anheuser Busch's twelve U.S.-based brewery facilities? Or, for that matter, why wouldn't he pick a famous international brewery such as Bass from Burton-on-Trent, Guinness from Dublin, Sapporo from Tokyo, or Spaten from Munich?

His answer is clear and unambiguous: "Because the people at Sierra Nevada have committed themselves to quality and integrity," he says. "They pay attention to every detail. No expenses are spared. You see it wherever you go, from the polished wood paneling at the bar to the immaculately clean brewing equipment." All this adds up to its defining asset: "They consciously follow a long line of beer-making tradition. They know their history."

What tradition? Whose history? To discover what is so singular about Sierra Nevada, clearly I will need to delve deeper into this tradition, indeed into beer history, and try to understand the contradictions discussed at our lunchtime conversation. On my drive back to Chico, three questions begin to materialize: (1) Why are big industrial brewers in the U.S. reviled and respected with equal doses of passion? (2) Why does beer (alcohol in general) generate both animosity and adulation from the general public? (Certain religions forbid it outright; certain societies have experimented with outlawing it, as did the U.S. during Prohibition from 1920–1933; conversely, other societies have practically enshrined it into their cultural and political framework, as is the case with the German Beer Purity Law known as Reinheitsgebot). (3) Why would a leading beer expert nominate an American craft brewery as the world's leading practitioner of quality and integrity? Wasn't America supposed to be the arch-nemesis of beer quality?

These are big questions, bigger possibly than the ones I asked in the introduction to this book and I certainly don't want to get out of my depth. Nevertheless, I realize that a broader historical perspective is in order before I begin to tell the story of Sierra Nevada Brewing Co.

"I'VE SAID IT ALL WHEN I'VE SAID BUD"

WHEN I first arrived in the States in August 1977, the generally-accepted criticism of American beer was that it suffered from being bland, sugary and over-carbonated. Typical were the complaints of Pulitzer Prize-winning columnist Mike Royko for the *Chicago Tribune*, who was equally obsessed with the poor quality of beer in the U.S. as other pressing issues of the time, notably Watergate and the Vietnam War. America, he proclaimed, made "the world's worst beer." It was, he said, "Our national shame." With sad resignation, he admitted: "I have tried them all. I've popped the top and twisted the cap. ... I've said it all when I've said Bud."

Royko delivered a stinging condemnation of American brewing: "Regardless of what label or slogan you choose, it all tastes as if the secret brewing process involves running it through a horse." Such a sad state of affairs forced him to raise an uncomfortable question: "Why is our beer so bad that young people are being driven to drinking Apple Dapple?"

His answer: cost-cutting. "It is cheaper to make this kind of beer," he concluded. Hence the use of inferior barley and hops mixed with cereal adjuncts such as corn or rice. To compensate for the poor quality of their beer, brewers resorted to slick advertising. His ensuing insight was both astute and amusing: "So when you open a can of beer, half your money is paying for the sickly fluid it contains. And the other half is paying for the ad that convinces you how good it is."

I vividly remember these slick, ingenious advertising slogans from the late '70s and early '80s: while Anheuser-Busch informed me that Budweiser was "the King of Beers," Miller suggested "If you've got the time, we've got the beer," and Schlitz reminded me that "When you're out of Schlitz, you're out of Beer." Later, Coors would proudly announce it was "Brewed with Pure Rocky Mountain Spring Water." But the most pervasive (and invasive) ad campaign was the "Great Taste ... Less Filling" slogan that seemed to catch the American imagination in the 1970s and helped to increase sales of Miller Lite fourfold from 1973 to 1978. Notwithstanding the creativity of these commercials, the sober reality was that behind such advertising rhetoric, American beer was still the laughing-stock of beer connoisseurs around the world and "piss and vinegar" was the commonly used epithet to describe its insipid flavor.

By the late 1970s, Royko's complaints had not gone unheeded. In fact, his criticism seemed to serve as a wake-up call for baby-boomer homebrewers who were coming of age. In an essay entitled "Extreme Brewing in America," Sam Calagione, owner of Dogfish Head Craft Brewery in Delaware, looks back in appreciation at the first generation of craft brewers who paved the way for his own brand of extreme brewing: "These brewers were telling their fellow Americans to wake up—you have taste buds—you have a mind—you know what you want to drink more than your television or a billboard does" (89). Topping the list in his pantheon of names are Ken Grossman, Fritz Maytag, Jack McAuliffe, Bert Grant, Jim Koch, Garret Oliver, and Charlie Papazian.

Calagione's central hypothesis is that these brewers were not only reviving old crafts and skills, but were doing so in a uniquely American tradition that highlighted innovation, experimentation, and imagination. He writes: "It was time to recreate a tradition that reflected the greater American tradition—because tradition is nothing more than a series of experiments that have proven to work. And, as Americans, experimenting is what we do best" (89).

It's a hypothesis also developed by beer historian, Maureen Ogle in her book, *Ambitious Brew*. "Beer's history," she argues, "embodies the essence of what it is to be American: our ambivalent attitude toward alcohol, our passion for invention and creativity, and our seemingly limitless ability to take old ideas and things and remake them in our uniquely American image" (ix).

According to Ogle, the story of American beer is marked by three predominant themes: the successful blending of tradition and innovation, the impact of immigration, and the legacy of the temperance movement. And in Chico, home to Sierra Nevada Brewing Co, the strands are intricately connected in a way that merits closer examination.

But first, some world historical context.

JOHN BARLEYCORN, PINK BOOTS, AND PILGRIMAGES

BEER INSPIRES fear and reverence in equal measure. Perhaps this is because of the mysterious alchemy that transforms grain into alcohol. Or perhaps it's because of beer's ability to affect our moods and perceptions with significant power. The word "ale," after all, derives from the old Saxon word "alu," which can mean either religious ecstasy or disturbing hallucination. Fear of the beverage often gets channeled into strict laws, codes, and prohibitions. But if we turn to myth, we find a different story—one that often emphasizes reverence sometimes bordering on religious zeal.

A popular folk song in my university days, "John Barleycorn," captures this paradox with haunting power. It tells the story of a grain god, John Barleycorn, who is brutally victimized by a fearful mob. He is literally pulped into a mash. But he lives on as a fermented drink, for others to enjoy. On the one hand, the song can be interpreted as a priggish manifesto against beer consumption—all the fury and animosity towards the alcoholic grain is taken out on a symbolic figurehead who is hounded and beaten to death. On the other hand, it's also a raucous drinking song. At least, that's the way I remember it, as belted out by two legendary folk rock bands of the 1970s, Traffic and Jethro Tull. The song ends with an ironic twist:

> Well, they have worked their will on John Barleycorn,
> But he lived to tell the tale,
> For they pour him out of an old brown jug,
> And they call him home brewed ale.

I've always found it difficult not to listen to this song without wanting to raise a glass to salute the enduring qualities of beer in the ebb and flow of history.

In fact, beer is as old as civilization, possibly predating bread, its grain-based cousin. It has been consumed for over 6,000 years. Ancient Assyrians, Sumerians, Babylonians, and Chinese, all made beer although it was unhopped and considerably sweeter. The Sumerians worshipped a brewing goddess named Ninkasi and sang a hymn in her honor that reads in part:

> Ninkasi, when you pour out the filtered beer of the vat
> It is like the flow of the Tigris and Euphrates.

In ancient Egypt, the mother of all deities, Hathor, was famous for organizing wild and ecstatic New Year celebrations involving copious amounts of red-barley beer or *boosa* (from which the word "booze" derives). Three thousand years later, beer guilds such as the Pink Boots Society and Ales for Females continue the work of Ninkasi and Hathor by promoting careers for women in the beer world and smashing the myth that brewing belongs exclusively to the province of men. Pink Boots founder Teri Fahrendorf believes there should be no glass ceiling for women in the world of brewing and travels around the country, touring breweries (including Sierra Nevada) to make her case.

In the ancient Mesopotamian epic, *Gilgamesh,* beer serves as an important catalyst in humanity's perennial fight against evil in the world. After consuming seven jugs of beer, the savage beast, Enkidu, is transformed into a gallant and civilized nobleman. "He was elated and his face glowed," the narrator tells us. As the beer gradually takes effect, the beast loses his wicked ways "and became expansive and sang with joy!" He joins forces with the gallant hero, Gilgamesh, and they subsequently go on a quest to do battle against demons and monsters from the netherworld.

It's no coincidence that beer often takes center stage in the mythology of cultures from around the world. The national epic of Finland, *The Kalevala,* pays tribute to beer's uplifting effects in its opening lines:

> *Bring me too a cup of strong-beer.*
> *It will add to our enchantment,*
> *To the pleasure of the evening.*

The saga tells the story of a female brewer, Osmotar (another role model for the Pink Boots Society, perhaps?) whose preparations for an upcoming wedding involve brewing the perfect batch of beer (described in painstaking detail in over 400 verses). This beer, called Kalew, was famous because it could "fill the heart with joy and gladness, fill the mind with wisdom-sayings, (and) fill the tongue with ancient legends."

The early Germanic cultures of central and northern Europe attributed magical powers to ale runes—inscriptions on the inside of drinking vessels. These runes fended off the enemy and carried the message that fermented drinks were gifts from the gods, no less.

Beowulf, the oldest poem in the English language, takes place mainly in King Hrothgar's Great Hall where cups of mead-ale are regularly drunk in order to stave off the dark Scandinavian winters. The hall is attacked by an archenemy, Grendel, who is not only deeply envious of the civilized comforts he discovers there but is also eager to try some hearty brew for himself. Underneath his monstrous exterior, it turns out, is just another beer connoisseur in the making.

And then there's Geoffrey Chaucer's medieval magnum opus, *The Canterbury Tales.* It's the story of thirty pilgrims who congregate for a few pints at The Tabard Inn, a pub whose original site still remains in Southwark, on the outskirts of London. They hatch plans to make the sixty-mile journey to Canterbury Cathedral on foot, taking turns to tell tales along the way. The portly, genial innkeeper, Harry Bailey, full of boozy mirth and jolliness, offers a free supper (and more pints) as a reward for the best tale. Perhaps the pilgrims paused at The Bishop's Finger pub in Canterbury for one last tipple before entering the sacred precincts of the cathedral. We never get to know who wins the storytelling contest in the end. It doesn't really matter because, like an enjoyable evening of social drinks, what's important is the journey itself rather than the destination.

Nowadays, you're likely to find as many visitors making pilgrimages to Chico as Canterbury, on a quest to see the famed copper kettles at Sierra Nevada and partake of the Taproom's exalted conviviality.

FROM TESGUINO TO BILLY BEER

WHEN DID beer arrive in the Americas? The usual response is: "on the *Mayflower* in 1620." Yet beer was a staple beverage amongst Native American tribes before the arrival of European settlers. Pueblo Indians of the Southwest used corn and juniper instead of barley and hops, and added a hint of mesquite, to brew *tesguino* beer for religious practices, rituals, and ceremonies. In Mesoamerica, the Aztecs favored another corn-based beer called *sendecho*, bittered with the tepozan plant.

True, it's likely that beer was a prized victual on board the *Mayflower*. One theory claims that the Pilgrims landed at Plymouth Rock rather than at the mouth of the Hudson River because they were concerned about running out of beer and wanted to make landfall as quickly as possible. Early colonial society was, according to some historians, not as prim and proper as we're led to believe. Most Puritans were homebrewers and adapted to what was available locally, so they brewed potions with corn, birch, and spruce rather than malt and hops. In 1636, when Harvard University was established, a regular supply of beer was provided to faculty and students by a brewhouse on campus. (John Harvard's Brew House remains a popular microbrewery restaurant in Boston's Harvard Square). Vassar Female College was established in 1861 from the proceeds of Hudson Valley Brewery, a successful business operated by an immigrant from England, Matthew Vassar.

The Founding Fathers were accomplished home brewers who, in addition to protesting taxes on tea, urged a boycott of English beer and cider—favoring homemade brews instead. George Washington adapted English porter, giving it distinctive American flavors and added spiciness—licorice and molasses. Thomas Jefferson brewed a ginger honey ale that he fermented with honey. James Madison made a dark wheat ale hand smoked with Virginia oak. Samuel Adams came from a family with a long tradition as malsters—preparing and supplying malt for brewers. Ironically, he was not a particularly successful brewer. (Now, his name is associated with the East Coast's most successful craft brewery).

By the time of the Civil War, there were more than 3,000

breweries in the U.S. producing close to four million barrels of beer a year.

Nineteenth century immigrants from Germany furthered this rich tradition by bringing with them new brewing tastes (lighter beer instead of heavy English ales), modern brewing techniques (refrigeration, cooling, and pasteurization), and a new bottom-fermenting yeast strain. Thus, they established a style of beer that remains America's favorite choice: a light-bodied, chilled, and carbonated lager, low in alcohol and bright yellow in color. The names of these early German beer pioneers still echo today in the companies they founded: Frederick Miller, Adolphus Busch, Eberhard Anheuser, Frederick Pabst, Joseph Schlitz, Adolph Coors. They helped to accelerate production of beer to forty million barrels a year by 1900 and established great brewing cities such as New York, Milwaukee, and St. Louis.

Meanwhile, in the Sierra Nevada foothills of northern California, the 1849 gold rush resulted in swelling numbers of out-of-state prospectors, and the birth of gold-mining towns, breweries, and bars. A new style of beer was pioneered—a hybrid that used lager yeast to ferment the wort at warmer ale temperatures thus releasing spurts of steam and carbon dioxide during the fermentation process. This became known as steam ale, a distinctive West Coast style, resurrected by Fritz Maytag a century later and, as we shall see in the next chapter, an inspiration for the microbrewing revolution in the early 1980s.

Anti-immigration prejudice at the end of the nineteenth century (particularly against the Irish and Germans) intermingled with a wider antipathy towards alcohol. The devil's drink was regarded by some as a threat to the American values of prudence, rectitude, and industry. The entry of the U.S. into World War One on the side of the Allies against Germany intensified the animosity. German-style lager, for example, became known derisively as "Kaiser brew." Finally, the 1920 National Prohibition Act (the Volstead Act) prohibited beverages containing more than .5 percent alcohol. "The Noble Experiment," as it was called, was designed to foster safer cities and workplaces, even a healthier nation, but it inadvertently created mobsters, racketeers, bootleggers, and a counterculture of crime and underground activity. Consumption of alcohol was driven underground into secretive speakeasies, saloons, and illegal breweries. The thirteen-year experiment devastated the brewing industry. In 1920, there were two thousand breweries. By 1933, when Prohibition ended with ratification of the Twenty-first Amendment, there were just 750. Many had stayed in business by producing either soft drinks or a drink that was euphemistically called "near beer."

The post-Prohibition era witnessed the rise of the industrial production of beer and its main conduit, the mega brewery. The old tied system was dismantled (whereby beer maker and retailer had been locked together in a forced relationship). Instead, a three-tier system was established consisting of beer maker, distributor, and retailer. Consequently, two new necessities came into play for the successful beer maker: firstly, you needed to be able to create a wider market for your product (mainly in bottles) and secondly, you needed to be able to deliver beer to that market. According to Maureen Ogle, nobody understood this new business model better than August A. Busch: "He used the noble experiment as a school in which to learn a new way of doing business" (20). Within a decade of the end of Prohibition, Anheuser-Busch was the world's largest brewing company.

In the course of the next five decades, the market share of the five largest U.S. breweries rose from around 15 percent to 95 percent. Beer went the way of fast food, becoming homogenized, highly processed, and industrialized. A sophisticated system of national distribution networks that made use of the newly constructed interstate highway system added to the efficiency of this new system of production. The explosion of television popularity, meanwhile, allowed for effective national advertising. It was the birth of sugary, bland, flavorless, and streamlined American beer.

By the time I arrived in the United States in 1977, the "Great Taste, Less Filling" craze had created a surge in popularity of lite beers that boasted only 70–100 calories and a low malt and hop profile. Described as "clean" and "refreshing," this is what Americans really wanted, apparently.

Or was it?

A counterrevolution was gathering force, both in culinary and drinking circles, demanding more to life than Wonder bread and Bud Light. Looking back, it's tempting to consider Mike Royko the spokesman for this disenchanted generation. His sentiments were echoed and amplified by Charles McCabe in a *San Francisco Chronicle* column published on September 13, 1979: "The rebellious young seem to feel that our beer, like practically everything else in our society, is a bit phony. That there is something better that has escaped their grasp. It excites their curiosity."

When President Jimmy Carter legalized homebrewing in 1979, he finally granted permission for this generation to indulge their passion without breaking the law. But President Carter was better known in beer circles for having a lager-loving brother, Billy, in whose name a beer was made by Falls City Brewing Company. For a short while in the late '70s, Billy Beer enjoyed a faddish following but its popular shine, like that of the president's brother, quickly faded. Maybe, after all, Americans wanted flavor and character in their beer, not gimmickry.

In the same year that President Carter legalized homebrewing, Fritz Maytag addressed the annual convention of the Brewers Association of America: "Perhaps there is a change in the air," he noted modestly. "In talking to many people around the country I see what I think is a growing appreciation of the small brewery." At that very moment in Chico, California, two young entrepreneurs originally hailing from Los Angeles made the decision to open one such small brewery, naming it after a nearby mountain range, Sierra Nevada.

CHICO CULTURE AND COUNTERCULTURE

W HY DID these two young men choose Chico? And what are the special qualities that make this relatively small and remote northern California town—90 miles north of Sacramento, 175 miles northeast of San Francisco—a prominent fixture on the world beer map?

First, there's the water, of course. Like most famous beer towns, Chico has a reliable and abundant supply, thanks to the Tuscan Aquifer—a vast reservoir of water that lies beneath Chico. Importantly, the water profile is clean, benign, and easily modified to suit different styles of ales and lagers.

Second, there is what the Chamber of Commerce likes to call Chico's "special ambiance." The city's name means "young boy" in Spanish. It is located in the northern reaches of California's Sacramento Valley, nestled between two sets of mountain ranges: the Coastal Range to the west and the Sierra Nevada to the east. It's a medium size city with a population of close to 90,000. Blessed with a hot Mediterranean climate and sunshine almost year-round, it is still less than a two-hour drive from snow-covered mountains. It has one of the largest municipal parks in the nation (3,670 acres) extending five miles from downtown into surrounding foothills (with horseback and hiking trails, barbecue pits, deep swimming holes, even a forty-acre Frisbee golf course). During the hot months of summer, farmer's markets and evening concerts in the open-air City Plaza are major draws. As one observer puts it, "To say Chico is laid-back is like saying Texans wear big hats." Another comments: "Chico is a town where hippy casualties from the 1960s just about keep up with the leisurely pace of life." It's no accident that it's celebrated as one of the nation's most bicycle-friendly cities and that *American Cowboy Magazine* rated it the "Top Place to Live the Western Dream" in 2010.

Third, this stretch of the Sacramento Valley has a legacy of innovation and experimentation that can be traced back to Chico's founding by General John Bidwell, an early settler who discovered gold on the Feather River in 1848 thus helping to prompt the Gold Rush. Before settlers arrived, the area was populated by Mechoopda Maidu Indians; they called it Tadoiko and, according to local legend, it was created when Earth Maker and Turtle came ashore on a raft. With his new wealth, Bidwell purchased a 28,000-acre allotment of land—Rancho del Arroyo Chico. On this land, he built an Italianate mansion, planted close to four hundred varieties of nuts and fruits, and laid out the city of Chico as a rectangular grid of fifty blocks. It was incorporated in 1872. The first building in the city was a saloon, on the corner of Main and Third. To this day, downtown is favored with coffee shops, funky murals, art benches, vintage clothing stores, and a slew of bars and restaurants. At the heart is City Plaza Park, a square whose original elms, planted by Bidwell, have recently been replaced by quick-growing shade trees.

Just north of Chico, in the town of Vina, a similar agricultural experiment to Bidwell's was conducted by Leland Stanford, railroad magnate and former governor of California. His Great Vina Ranch was, at the time of its completion in 1881, the world's largest vineyard at 35,000 acres. A century later, it passed into the hands of Trappist monks and became the first Cistercian winery in North America. New Clairvaux Vineyard, as it's called, is currently collaborating with Sierra Nevada Brewing Co. to produce a series of Belgian-style beers, available in 2011.

Throughout the twentieth century, the Central Valley of California was to become a testing ground for agricultural and technological innovations. A system of dams, aqueducts, and levees created pasture out of semi-desert and allowed for passage of water from the north state to the arid south; hybrid strains of plants—rice, kiwi, olives, almonds, peaches—were developed so as to suit hot, dry summers. Large-scale mechanized agriculture intermingled with small-scale organic farming. In this way, the "Inland Empire" developed into a technological miracle; some went so far as to call it "the garden of the world."

In 1868, John Bidwell married Annie Kennedy, daughter of a wealthy Whig politician from Washington, D.C. The influence of Annie Bidwell on her husband as well as on the future of the city is legendary. After marrying John, she demanded that all grapevines be torn out of their garden and that her husband should renounce the devil's drink for the rest of his life. She encouraged him to run for president as leader of the anti-alcohol Prohibition Party in the 1892 general election. (He eventually received 270,000 votes, the equivalent of 2.2 percent of the national vote). After his death in 1900, she became active in the local branch of the American Christian Temperance Union and a leader in the women's suffrage movement.

John and Annie Bidwell: Chico's founders. Courtesy of California State Parks.

It's easy to dismiss Annie's beliefs as prudish and singularly Victorian. Alcohol, she believed, ruined lives, damaged families, and discouraged a strong work ethic. But behind her stiff, uncompromising exterior lurked a complex and conflicted personality. Her stance against alcohol can partly be explained by the tragic fate of her only brother, Joey, who, at the age of fifty-two, slipped into the Patapsco River, Baltimore, in a state of hopeless intoxication. For much of his adult life, he had been haunted by the demon of drink. The lesson of his tragic life was not lost on Annie.

In fairness, her zeal for temperance was matched equally by a passion for education and a love of nature. In 1887, the Bidwells donated ten acres of land to secure a new state teacher's college, Chico Normal School, which later became California State University, Chico, where I currently teach. It's a pleasant residential campus of 16,000 students spread across 120 acres adjacent to downtown. After arriving here in 1988, I sometimes wondered if I had fallen down a rabbit-hole and entered a Norman Rockwell painting. Or was it Shangri-La? It was not unusual to see colleagues teaching in Birkenstocks and shorts. I noticed that students liked to talk a lot, resented lectures, and assumed it was okay to address their professors by their first name. Over the years, I've learned to wear shorts and sandals on campus, to smile more than I am accustomed to doing. I've even come to understand what it means to be "laid-back," if only in the theoretical sense.

Annie Bidwell will be remembered for one more important contribution. After her husband's death, she deeded a further 2,200 acres to the city of Chico. The appropriately named Bidwell Park consists of two sections. Lower Bidwell Park comprises valley oaks and lush riparian vegetation that provide an inviting canopy of shelter from the scorching summer sun. (It also served as a film set for the 1939 Hollywood version of *The Adventures of Robin Hood*, starring Errol Flynn). Upper Bidwell Park reaches into the Sierra Nevada foothills, its rugged canyons carved by glaciers, creeks, and ancient volcanic flows. The most controversial regulation stipulated by Annie—still in place today although erratically enforced—was that there should be no "intoxicating liquors of any kind" in the park.

Abundant water, lots of sunshine, spectacular outdoor scenery, and a quirky history. That's what awaited seventeen-year-old Ken Grossman when he first visited Chico in the summer of 1972. He entertained some vague ideas about fixing bikes and making beer on the side. Yet he ended up having the most telling impact on the local community since the Bidwells a century earlier, and a not inconsiderable impact on the history of beer in the United States, indeed the world.

Scenes from the Taproom, Part I
January 4, 2008: Shelter from the Storm

The worst storm in twenty years is sweeping through the Pacific Northwest, toppling giant redwoods, downing power lines, and leaving two million people throughout northern California without electricity. In darkened Chico, streetlights are out, intersections snarled, grocery-store parking lots eerily empty. The mayor has declared a state of emergency, requesting special resources from out-of-town relief agencies. Within days, the event has become the stuff of local legend known simply as "The Great Storm of 2008."

But, on this day, the lights are shining in the Taproom bar at the town's Sierra Nevada Brewing Co. Regulars and employees toast their good fortune while voicing anxious concern for the safety of friends and family.

Among them: Alan Judge, Sierra Nevada filtration specialist, who sips contentedly from a pint of Sierra Nevada Pale Ale. He's warm, dry, and among friends. He sits at the end of the long bar and surveys the familiar décor around him: the polished wood countertop, the sixteen beer taps, and the impressive Sierra Nevada logo backlit behind the bar featuring a mountain stream cascading from snow-capped peaks framed by garlands of hops and barley. In the open plan kitchen behind him, cooks are chopping, stirring, and mixing while chatting away merrily; occasionally, one of them uses a long-armed spatula to feed pizzas into the brick oven. The storm rages outside, but here he's surrounded by high spirits.

Another workweek is over, and Alan—a transplant from Liverpool, avid soccer player, and respected local musician—is doing what he usually does on Friday evenings, relaxing at Sierra Nevada's Taproom while downing a few pints of strong-bodied beer.

Tonight is different. While the Taproom and adjoining Restaurant regularly bustle on Fridays with locals and out-of-towners, tonight friends and families linger longer over their pints and pizzas. Strangers are chatting like old acquaintances. No one seems eager to leave this oasis of comfort and light.

Soon, Alan is joined by colleagues from other departments of the brewery: fermentation, bottling, packaging, R&D. They banter with Nick, the lanky bartender, and Jessica, the friendly waitress, staying until closing time, 10.00 P.M., when they fan out through a darkened town, most returning to homes that will stay without heat and power for several days. But for now, at least, they are warmed by their evening at the brewery, flooded with light and laughter.

In fact, on this historic day, Sierra Nevada is one of the few places open for business in the northern reaches of California's Central Valley, also known as the Sacramento Valley. Most businesses in the area are shut down completely unless they are equipped with emergency back-up generators or are lucky enough to have escaped the destructive fury of the storm altogether. Unique among major breweries and indeed among almost all businesses of its size, Sierra Nevada has achieved over 90 percent energy self-sufficiency. That, coupled with its emergency diesel generators, enables it to be entirely decoupled from the local electric company's vulnerable infrastructure when needed. Just four months earlier, Sierra Nevada had begun to generate energy from a three-acre solar array that, along with the operation of one of the largest hydrogen fuel cell installalations in the world, has helped to move the brewery toward the eventual goal of becoming entirely energy independent.

Sierra Nevada Brewing Co. is not just a producer of good beers and bonhomie. It is a physical space—like any good pub it provides shelter from the storm. And in times of adversity, it's always there, come hell or high water.

CHAPTER TWO

The Making of a Dream and the Birth of a Beer
1972–1980

BEER, BIKES, AND A VOLKSWAGEN BUS

O N A summer afternoon in 1972, seventeen-year-old Ken Grossman and three buddies from Los Angeles were enjoying a three-day cycling tour along the Pacific coastline from Ukiah to Monterey. They stopped for a beer at a bar a few miles south of Santa Cruz on Highway 1. They were tired, hungry, and thirsty. Apparently looking old enough to pass for twenty-one, the teenagers were served bottles of Anchor Steam beer, brewed one hundred miles up the coast in the North Beach neighborhood of San Francisco.

The taste of Anchor Steam was a revelation for Grossman and his thirsty companions. It was more flavorful and sophisticated than the usual industrial beer on the market. It tasted somewhere between ale and lager: creamy, rich and robust, with a fizzy head although not overly carbonated. Satisfied and fortified, they resumed riding down to Monterey where they loaded their bikes into a pickup truck and drove back to Los Angeles, their hometown.

This brief visit made a lasting impression on Grossman, one

he would carry with him for years, and that he continues to recall with fondness. He understood for the first time that an American company was producing and selling good beer, really good beer, the kind previously available only as expensive imports or as an exceptional home brew. This revelation ended up having a significant impact on the history of beer brewing in the United States.

Like most fanatical homebrewers, young Grossman was familiar with the story of Anchor Brewing Company, although he had yet to enjoy its new steam beer. The brewery was owned by Fritz Maytag, a Stanford graduate with a taste for the finer things in life. In 1965, Maytag had purchased the seventy-year-old brewery with money inherited from his family's washing machine business. His goal was "to make the best beer in the world," using high quality two-row barley along with whole hops, something major American breweries were not doing. By the early 1970s Maytag had perfected a steam brewing technique, blending Old and New World brewing styles. Pitching lager yeast at warmer temperatures, and then fermenting the beer in shallow two feet deep vessels before using flash pasteurization for short bursts of fifteen seconds rather than fifteen minutes, he produced signature spurts of steam and carbon dioxide when the beer was tapped.

Maytag's passion for traditional ales was shared by an increasing number of Americans, including Ken Grossman. Since his early teens, Grossman had been fascinated by the alchemy of beer brewing. While most junior high and high school students learned chemistry by studying textbooks and memorizing abstract formulae, Grossman conducted his own style of lab experiments by assisting the father of his best friend, Gregg Moeller, to concoct various types of alcohol, mainly wine and beer. The Moeller family lived a few doors down from the Grossmans in Woodland Hills (a residential suburb in northeast Los Angeles). The two Grossman brothers (Ken and eldest brother, Steve) would often sneak around and drink some of Mr. Moeller's beer. If they were lucky, they might get their hands on some Ballantine IPA, probably the nation's best noncommercial beer available at the time. Mr. Moeller was a rocket scientist by day, but a zealous homebrewer after hours. "He'd always have jugs fermenting in the porch and all sorts of exotic aromas," Grossman recalls. "He was boiling something on the stove every weekend. And so it piqued my interest at a pretty young age." Later, Moeller senior was to become one of the original members of the Maltose Falcons, founded in 1974, and self-described as "the world's oldest homebrewing club."

Grossman's parents were hardly thrilled about the neighborhood shenanigans, but indulged their adventurous sons nonetheless. Before long, young Ken went one step further and crafted a beer-making facility in his bedroom. At the age of sixteen, he read Fred Eckhardt's seminal book *A Treatise on Lager Beers: A Handbook for Americans and Canadians on Lager Beer* (1970) and was inspired to try out a recipe. For his first batch of homemade beer, he mixed one can of Blue Ribbon hop-flavored malt syrup with four pounds of sugar and warm water, then added a pack of Red Star cake yeast.

If it sounds no more complicated than making a pot of tea (at least from a layman's point of view), then that's because in the early days of homebrewing—given the lack of supplies and equipment—the process of making beer was essentially the same as making a pot of tea (minus the yeast, of course): you poured hot water over the malt mash (like pouring hot water over tea leaves), then you lautered the spent malt (straining the tea leaves), and finally you let it steep for a while, adding hops to the brew for extra flavor (or a few leaves of mint, in the case of tea). A couple of teaspoons of sugar thrown in for good measure and Bob's your uncle, you've made the perfect brew (or as my dad used to say, "a lovely cuppa!").

Ken was the middle child and, in his own words, "a bit of

a juvenile delinquent." To this day, his mother, Eleanor, recalls how she had to "Kenny-proof" everything in the house while he was growing up because "he was always doing a dozen things at one time." By the age of fifteen, she tells me with a mixture of resignation and breathless admiration, his completed construction projects included: a photography darkroom in the garage, an underground fort with its own air inlet, a fully wired two-story tree house (which proved a popular hangout for the neighborhood kids), and a go-kart track around the home's half-acre backyard. Given these precedents, it didn't seem so strange that her son would eventually attempt to build a mini-brewery in his bedroom! Of course, as a carryover from the Prohibition era, homebrewing was still technically illegal, especially for an underage junior high student. "I was not pleased," Eleanor recalls. "I don't approve of drinking, and I especially don't condone it in children. But at the same time, I wanted to encourage Ken's creativity. Fortunately, his early beer was undrinkable. Most of it got dumped."

Grossman graduated from Taft High School in May 1972. But rather than attend the graduation ceremony, he spent the weekend backpacking in nearby hills. He had not yet decided what he wanted to do with his life. "I was not much of an academic," he admits freely. He disliked chemistry and was not interested in studying science unless it had a practical application. His favorite school subject was photography—most likely because his teacher was a member of the Sierra Club and frequently took his students on hikes and bike rides to nearby scenic areas. Learning by the book had been a constant struggle for Grossman; he was far more comfortable learning through trial and error and by hands-on exploration.

Brother Steve recalls when he first realized that there was something special about Ken's aptitude for practical problem solving. It was during his senior year at Taft High School and he had, as usual, driven Ken, fifteen, and a couple of neighbors to school in his 1959 Renault Dauphine. Halfway through morning classes, Steve was summoned to the parking lot where he discovered his car engulfed in flames. As it turned out, Ken had a penchant for smoking Hav-a-Tampa Jewels cigars and had accidentally left a smoking butt in the back seat that morning. The car burned to the ground leaving a fragile metal circle and gaunt metal rod where there had once been a steering wheel and gear stick. The brothers managed to get the burned-out shell of a car back home where it was duly converted into a destruction derby-car for their go-kart track!

But Ken now owed his brother a big favor and so when Steve's next car (a 1962 Austin Healey 3000) had a problem engaging first gear, it fell to fifteen-year-old Ken to rebuild the transmission. He did so without the benefit of an owner's manual. The only problem—now reverse gear didn't engage properly. So Ken rebuilt the transmission over, once again through sheer instinct rather than going by the book. This time, all the gears worked fine. As Steve tells me this story, I notice a good-humored sparkle in his eye. But he quickly turns serious. "Ken is probably the best mechanical engineer in the brewery business," he says adamantly.

If anyone deserves credit for fostering young Ken Grossman's genius with tools—it is most likely another neighbor, John Hungerford, who lived in the house directly across the street. Hungerford was a school principal whose favorite hobby was to do repair jobs around the house. According to Steve Grossman, he owned "every tool imaginable in his shop." He had "thousands and thousands of tools" tidily stored away in neat rows all under lock and key. Hungerford's son, another of Ken's buddies, allowed Ken to "borrow" tools whenever he wanted. Once the father discovered that his tools were disappearing on a regular basis, he threw a fit and immediately put an end to the free loan service. Later in life, Mr. Hungerford visited Chico and was duly impressed with the Sierra Nevada brewing facility. By that time, of course, he had forgiven Ken for his past trespasses, and even acknowledged the fortuitous role he had undoubtedly played in contributing to Grossman's hands-on education.

While his buddies were preparing to go to university in the summer of 1972, Grossman didn't even bother to send out applications, and was not particularly interested in attending college. When one of his friends suggested they embark on a bike tour along the Pacific coast, he was happy to go along. He hoped that the adventure might help to clarify his life goals. By serendipity, another breakthrough event happened later that same summer of 1972. He visited a college town in northern California sandwiched between the Coast Range and the Sierra Nevada mountains, a pretty little place with a cute Spanish name, Chico. Some of his friends, including Gregg Moeller, had been accepted into Chico State University.

While they attended freshman orientation sessions on campus, Grossman spent a couple of days exploring the Sacramento Valley town. If he could find a short-term job there, he thought, perhaps it could tide him over while he decided where his passions would take him in life. He inquired at various bike shops to see if they needed a mechanic and got an offer from an outfit called Village Cycles—a small, family-owned business located on one of the town's main business arteries. While beer and wine-making were hobbies he enjoyed, the geometry of bike mechanics also appealed to him. "Keep the job for me, I'll let you know shortly," he told the owners. He returned to his home in Woodland Hills and spent several days backpacking in the southern part of the Sierra while thinking through his options.

By the end of summer, Grossman had made his choice. The taste of Anchor Steam beer still lingered in his mouth, drawing him back to northern California. And the job offer at the bike store still stood.

On a cloudless August morning, his blue Volkswagen bus steamed out of Los Angeles on Interstate 5, bound for Chico 550

"Which way Chico?" Young Ken Grossman in the Sierra Nevada.

miles to the north. In the back of the vehicle, mixed in with his luggage, were an Italvega touring bike, various wrenches, a hydrometer, plastic buckets, hoses, and some cans of hop-flavored malt extract. Unlike his role model, Fritz Maytag, he didn't have much money. But that didn't matter. He was young, and life was an adventure.

Grossman's plan was to work at the cycle shop and take a few chemistry classes at Butte College, the local community college. These modest ambitions were adequate to sustain the seventeen-year-old's twin passions for fixing bikes and making beer.

As he steered into Chico in August 1972, Grossman could never have dreamed that three decades later he would be the owner of the largest business in town, one famous across the country and overseas for producing beers that would rival (and, in the opinion of many, surpass) the quality of Anchor Brewing Company. Nor could he have predicted that the microbrewing revolution which he helped to launch, along with fellow visionaries like Fritz Maytag, would fundamentally change the profile of American beer and the culture of beer drinking in the United States.

"A COOL TOWN"

THE VALLEY town that first impressed Ken Grossman in 1972 has historically held an ambivalent attitude towards alcohol, as noted in chapter one. Like many Gold Rush-era towns, its first business was a saloon, its second a church. Chico's founding father, General John Bidwell, was a moderate drinker until he met the woman who would become his wife, Annie Elliott Kennedy, and was forsworn to give up alcohol. The couples' attitude towards drink still influences the community: The five-mile-long Bidwell Park, their gift to Chico, observes strict regulations prohibiting the use of alcohol.

But Bidwell was also the prime mover in bringing a college to Chico, and with any college come youthful high jinks and a culture of parties and drinking. Chico State University is no different than other schools, and as a residential campus—most of its students come from elsewhere—located in an outdoorsy town with generally warm weather, it can't prevent young people from having the kind of alcohol-fueled fun college students everywhere enjoy.

The town continues to be a magnet for out-of-town revelers, particularly on holidays such as Halloween and St. Patrick's Day. The campus that Bidwell originally bequeathed to the state has acquired an infamous reputation for being one of the nation's "top party schools" (culminating in *Playboy* magazine's 1987 announcement that it was Number One).

Pioneer Week—a community event intended to celebrate the Wild West spirit—was a longtime Chico tradition that had been observed since 1917. On April 25, 1987, it turned riotous, with drunken students building bonfires in intersections and overturning cars. "Enough is enough," proclaimed the university president, Robin Wilson. "I'm going to take this thing out in the back yard and shoot it in the head." And so he did. The termination of Pioneer Week was swiftly followed by other measures to raise alcohol awareness on campus. For example, a new office called CADEC (Campus Alcohol and Drug Education Center) was established whose primary purpose was to educate students about substance abuse.

None of this stopped the partying, however. Halloween got even bigger, with thousands of students and out-of-towners swarming through downtown Chico decked out in bizarre costumes. If you were twenty-one and tipsy, it was self-indulgent fun, but if you were a police officer obliged to preserve public order, it was a disaster waiting to happen. The city cracked down, bringing in police from all over northern California and applying a zero tolerance policy to public drunkenness.

Despite the mayhem and debauchery, Grossman recalls his early days in Chico in the mid-1970s with fondness. "Back then, the town was pretty wild. Pioneer Week was in full swing. And that's one of the things that attracted me. Coming from L.A., where the police were unbelievably mean, and the Watts riots were a recent memory, it was interesting to see that block parties were somewhat sanctioned by the police. You could close your whole street off and have a huge party and the police would drive by. ... When the students were in town, it was a pretty wild atmosphere."

Grossman's second job, after a stint at Village Cycles, was at Pullins Cyclery. This was the oldest bike shop in town, housed in a brick building at the corner of Eighth Street and Broadway. By serendipity or coincidence, a century earlier it had been Chico's only brewery. A master brewer from Bavaria named Charles Croissant bought the building from John Bidwell in 1874. He paid the grand sum of one dollar for it. There he brewed, and served, ales, lagers, and porters for the next twenty-five years. In the rear, a saloon and card room did a roaring business. Upstairs, there was a boarding house. Because the building was located south of the town's newly incorporated boundaries, the Bidwells could only have looked on and frowned from the safe distance of their mansion.

The original Chico Brewery (run by Charles Croissant at the end of the nineteenth century) as featured on the bottle label of "Old Chico," a Sierra Nevada CrystalWheat beer only sold in Chico

In 1972, there were twelve thousand students on the Chico State campus; enrollment at nearby Butte College was two thousand but growing. The town's population at the time was thirty-five thousand, though the greater urban area was closer to fifty thousand. It was a small, comfortable town with a Norman Rockwell feel, notable for a lively downtown and for its proximity to spectacular scenic areas such as Mounts Lassen and Shasta. Protecting the area's natural resources remained a top priority for policy makers: it was one of the first cities in the nation to declare itself a Nuclear Free Zone and, in the early '80s it went on to establish a Green Line that restricted developers from building on surrounding farm land.

Grossman enjoyed exploring the more remote corners of the expanded 3,700-acre Bidwell Park. "Once the students left town in the summer, Chico became a sleepy town," he remembers. "You could go up into Upper Park and there would be no one."

He spent hours hiking its many trails and, after working up a good sweat, he'd dive into one of the many spectacular swimming holes along the creek. He became a member of Chico Velo, a loosely structured bike club whose mantra was "eat, breathe, drink, and pedal." It was alternatively known as "Mellow Velo" or "Spokes and Tokes." In the spirit of the times, bike rides took the form of organized anarchy: groups of friends cycled into the foothills or along the valley floor, later rewarding themselves with food, drink, and the occasional illicit substance.

In short, Chico was far from being the backward farm town characterized by San Francisco columnist Herb Caen who had famously commented, "Chico is the kind of town where Velveeta is kept in the gourmet section of the supermarket." That was enough to seal Chico's reputation as "the Velveeta capital of the world." Many Chicoans bristled at the sneer and felt that their town had been badly misunderstood. It was difficult not to take the Velveeta jibe personally. Yet they were to have the last laugh, for Chico would soon become known as the home of Sierra Nevada Brewing Co., producers of some of the best beer in the country, if not the world.

BIKES OR BEER?

GROSSMAN ENJOYED working at the bicycle shop. He soon earned the nickname "Dr. Kenny" from clients because of his mechanical skills. At the same time, he continued to learn all he could about brewing beer—not only the brewing process but also the engineering and architectural skills that were needed to construct a small-scale brewery.

Soon after his arrival in town, he embarked on a two-year chemistry program at Butte College. He enrolled in every class that would give him hands-on experience in the art and science of brewing: manufacturing brew kettles in a welding class, designing and constructing a lauter tun in agricultural mechanics, and conducting analysis on the quality of beer in his laboratory work.

One of the more bizarre experiments conducted by Grossman at the time involved converting a washer-dryer into a malt machine. Preparing malt is similar to washing and drying clothes, Grossman explains to me. First, you wash and soak the grain in water, and then you dry the germinated barley. Even though his hybrid machine (dubbed the "Malt Master Pro") never received a commercial patent, it clearly demonstrated that he had lost none of his childhood ingenuity and problem-solving genius.

Meanwhile, he was acquiring business skills as newly-promoted manager of Pullins Cyclery in Oroville, located twenty miles southeast of Chico. His boss ("Old Man Pullins" as he was affectionately called) recognized in Grossman a savvy entrepreneur, resourceful technician, and effective salesman.

But even though he was climbing the ranks of the biking hierarchy, his passion for making beer persisted. A nascent grassroots movement to legalize homebrewing would soon sanction an activity that Grossman had been performing for most of his young adult life. More important, it now paved the way for him, in 1976, at the age of twenty-one, to fulfill his dream of opening a business that would sell equipment and the finest ingredients for making homemade beer and wine.

The magnificent Malt Master Pro washing machine: an idea ahead of its time?

Homebrewing, by the mid-1970s, had become a nationwide fad. The Maltose Falcons, the first American homebrewing club, was established in 1974 in Los Angeles by Merlin Elhardt, and committed itself to brewing with all-grain batches and experimenting with various yeast cultures—in reaction to the industrialized techniques adopted by giant brewing companies. Grossman's neighbor, Cal Moeller, in Woodland Hills had been a founding member. The craze's momentum was carried throughout the 1970s by luminaries such as Charlie Papazian, founder of the American Homebrewers Association, and the British beer journalist, Michael Jackson, author of the groundbreaking *World Guide to Beer*. There was something faintly romantic about making your own beer; it seemed an honorable way of renouncing corporate values and embracing the "small is beautiful" mantra made popular by E. F. Schumacher in his 1973 book of the same name.

Homebrewing, observes Maureen Ogle "would ultimately serve as a breeding ground for microbrewing, nurturing the skills and ambitions of many of the people who later laid the foundation of (the) new brewing industry" (281).

Of course, Grossman cannot have known this in 1976 when he made the decision to try and eke a living out of the homebrewing mania. He quit Pullins and opened his new business, naming it simply The Home Brew Shop located downtown at 336 Broadway. For $60 a month, he rented a space in a warren of small indoor stores located on the second story of a downtown Chico business building. Known officially as the Upstairs Mall, it was popularly referred to as "the hippie emporium" by most of its customers. In addition to Grossman's home brew shop, the building contained a vintage-clothing store called Dreamweavers, a used-records store, a snacks-and-sandwiches joint called Oy Vey Bagels, and other small businesses trying to get by on the cheap. Grossman kept his own rent down by doing evening janitorial work for the landlord.

He traded his VW bus for a '57 Chevy truck, driving it regularly to Los Angeles and the San Francisco Bay Area to pick up supplies and equipment for his shop. The most perilous of these haulage trips involved stacking five-gallon glass carboys into pyr-

The Home Brew Shop: notice the wine-making wood barrel, five-gallon glass carboys, beer-making kits (containing malt extract, hops, and yeast), brew pots, plastic buckets, beer bottles, caps, tubing, hydrometer, and sanitizer.

amids on the flatbed of his truck and then driving four hundred miles on I-5, making sure not to hit any bumps along the way.

Meanwhile, he stayed enrolled at Butte College and took the occasional science class at neighboring Chico State.

It was natural that the woman he married shared his love of the outdoors. Her name was Katie Gonser, and she was—and still is—a tall, slender woman with a sprinkling of freckles and curly strawberry-blonde hair. Born and raised in Ames, Iowa, she maintains a midwestern love of wide spaces and big skies. They made a stunning couple, her fairness and delicate features contrasting with and complementing his solid, compact body, full brown beard, and high forehead.

On their very first date Ken and Katie hitched a ride to what later became the Ishi Wilderness Area and backpacked down into Deer Creek Canyon. The area is located northeast of Chico and is named after the last Stone Age Indian, who lived there with his tribe until everyone else was dead and then, in 1911, desperately alone and starving, he reluctantly joined civilization. There the couple enjoyed the solitude and beauty afforded by the deep canyon and its pristine mountain stream.

In early 1976, Ken and Katie married, and within a short time she was pregnant. Their first daughter was born in 1977. As a portent of things to come, they settled on the name, Sierra. Suddenly Grossman had a family and obligations, and he still had barely two nickels to rub together. "It was a real tough time," he now says.

Just as Katie shared Ken's interest in hiking and biking, she also shared the responsibility of raising a family and running a business together. She took a cradle into the The Home Brew Shop to look after baby Sierra, working three days a week from 10:00 to 6:00, while Ken took over the job for the other three days. On a good day, they might make $40. Meanwhile, on his days off, Ken continued to take classes at Butte Community College and to work one day a week at a new bike store called Chico Bike, owned by Dave Morrison. There, he befriended Steve O'Bryan and Ed McLaughlin—two luminaries who, in the course of the next three decades, were responsible for making Chico one of the most bike-friendly cities in the nation.

Bikes or beer? That was the question absorbing young Ken Grossman's mind. Should he play it safe and buy a bike shop in a town where his reputation as "Dr. Kenny" guaranteed him a steady stream of customers? Or should he try something more ambitious by using his experience at The Home Brew Shop to go the next step and open a microbrewery, just as Fritz Maytag had done years earlier in San Francisco?

Daughter Sierra and Ken Grossman's Chevy Truck

GILMAN WAY AND THE FIRST BATCH OF BEER: NOVEMBER 15, 1980

ONE OF the brew shop's customers was Paul Camusi. He was an avid biker, a fellow Los Angelino whose appreciation of So Cal culture set him apart from most Chicoans. After graduating from California State University, Northridge, in 1974, he spent a couple of years managing and upgrading apartment buildings in Los Angeles before moving to northern California. Like Grossman, he was a passionate homebrewer. In particular, he was fascinated by the microbiology of fermentation and the propagation of yeast cultures. They were introduced together by Ken's elder brother, Steve, also a cycling and home brew enthusiast.

Grossman and Camusi made a good team. While Grossman was a gifted problem solver and brilliant mechanic, Camusi had smart business sense. Soon they started attending weekend brewing seminars together at the University of California at Davis led by Professor Michael J. Lewis. Lewis was impressed by the intense fervor displayed by Grossman and Camusi and granted them access to an extensive library of journals and books on brewing. Even though the archive was mainly from the 1940s, '50s, and '60s, it gave the Chicoans valuable guiding principles for brewing commercial lagers and ales within a long historical tradition.

Lewis also identified his best graduate students and two in particular gravitated toward Grossman and Camusi—Michael Poley and Doug Muhleman. The foursome consulted frequently and kept in constant contact throughout the next four decades, despite going in opposite directions in brewing circles. Poley and Muhleman went on to work for Anheuser-Busch InBev, the largest corporate brewer in the world, one as senior resident brewmaster in Fairfield and the other as business manager in St. Louis.

In 1976 another microbrewery, New Albion Brewing Company, opened in Sonoma, California, in the heart of wine country, and this one soon caught the eye of beer advocates around the nation. Committed equally to the use of top-quality ingredients (name-brand yeast, superior malt, whole hops, and pure water) and to the avoidance of extracts or additives, it eventually became, as one observer put it, "the most important failed brewery in the industry's history." Its founder and owner was Jack McAuliffe, "an ornery and rough guy," says Grossman. Yet McAuliffe was generous in giving big brotherly advice (as well as stern warnings) to the two upstarts from Chico who visited New Albion shortly after its inauguration. They were impressed that McAuliffe had assembled a small brewery (with a capacity for brewing 450 barrels a year) out of recycled machines and equipment. His brewhouse vessels and fermenters were cobbled out of 55-gallon steel drums; his bottle washer was recycled from battleship decking. The total cost: $35,000. To further cut expenses, McAuliffe lived in a converted loft above the brewery. One of his admonitions made a particularly strong impression on Grossman: "Don't bother to get into this business unless you're going to invest in the things that are important."

According to Maureen Ogle, the combined examples offered by Fritz Maytag and Jack McAuliffe provided the impetus for the start of the craft brewing movement in the late '70s. Whereas Maytag had demonstrated that there was a market for resurrecting an old style of beer like Anchor Steam, McAuliffe "demonstrated that it was possible to build a brewery from scratch using scrap metal and salvaged equipment" (299). McAuliffe was, in the words of *Washington Post* journalist, Greg Kitsock, "A modern-day Moses (who) pointed the way but never entered the Promised Land himself."

Grossman and Camusi were ready to pursue the challenge of starting their own brewery in the foothills of northern California. Says Grossman: "When we came back from New Albion, we said, 'Yeah, this is something we can put together.' He [Camusi] was a serious homebrewer, and I was fairly handy; I could weld, so we felt we could put this operation together." More start-ups were coming on the scene: notably DeBakker Brewing Company in Novato and Boulder Brewing Company in Colorado. This was enough to convince Grossman and Camusi that the time was right to push forward with their dream.

In late 1978, Grossman and Camusi started to talk in earnest about the sort of brewery they wanted to own. Their vision was quixotic: using two-row barley malts (as opposed to the orthodox quantity, six) and five times the average amount of whole hops, they intended to produce a beer that would rank alongside Anchor Steam and New Albion. They called themselves "Sierra Nevada Brewing Co." The appellation was Katie's idea: at this point in their lives, she and Ken harbored a vague desire to relocate to foothills east of Chico, and naming their company after the mountain range was seen as a way of bringing this dream to fruition.

But first they required seed money. Grossman had $3,000 in savings. He somehow managed to convince his father (who thought his son was "a little nuts") to invest $10,000 and squeezed $5,000 from his grandfather, a judge in the state courts system. "We initially figured we could build a brewery for $50,000 or $60,000," Grossman recalls. Camusi's parents also put up $15,000. They asked friends and even fellow cyclists to invest. Some had faith and put some money down. Jean Harvey, wife of Chico State history professor Chuck Harvey, offered a generous $10,000. Others balked. Says Charlie Geshekter, a colleague of Harvey's husband: "Jean was quietly chatting with me and wondered if I would be interested in investing a few thousand dollars in the brewery because she had already put money into it. I recalled those awful post-ride beers and looked at her like she was mad." (Geshekter later admitted to me, over a couple of pints at the Taproom, that he still rues the missed opportunity to lend money to a company that eventually became the city's most profitable and prestigious business).

As of August 31, 1979, they had raised enough money to get started. Grossman and Camusi assembled a business plan and scouted around for a location in Chico where they could fulfill their dreams of producing quality beer.

By today's standards, the business plan is lofty in ideals but thin on practical details. Grossman still chuckles at the mention of it. Under the heading of *Marketing Strategy*, it reads: "Sierra Nevada beer will be promoted in relationship to young-adult athletic events: bicycling, running, roller skating and soccer." As for *Promotion Strategy*, the young entrepreneurs were unabashedly starry-eyed: "The Sierra Nevada name will identify the beer with the local gold rush tradition, implying mountain-bred freshness and a romantic aura that will capture the imagination of the young adult market."

In order to run the day-to-day business, they divided their labor in recognition of their signal strengths—Camusi's business sense and Grossman's mechanical genius: "Mr. Camusi will supervise the brewery lab and sanitation in addition to sharing market-

Gilman Way then (above) and now: site of the original Sierra Nevada Brewing Co., now a tire warehouse. Notice that the number of the street address has changed.

ing activities with Mr. Grossman. Mr. Grossman will supervise the brewery process and plant and cooperate on marketing."

Their goal—to average a profit of $6,000 a month—would hopefully be enough to pay the rent, repay loans, invest in future expansion, and feed their families with whatever was left over.

Innocent as this business plan may seem now, Grossman and Camusi did, however, show remarkable prescience in one critical area: the overriding adherence to quality. Their advice for the small brewer: "His must be a specialty product. The quality must be high and have good taste. This is how he will survive against the large brewers."

If the romantic aura worked its magic, the young dreamers hoped to sell 250 cases of beer a month to retail market, 500 cases to bars and restaurants, and 750 cases to liquor stores.

In August 1979, with business plan in hand, they took out a rental option on a 3,000-square-foot warehouse in south on 2539 Gilman Way. The building now houses a Tire Center, and is re-named 2570 South Whitman Place. It's situated across the street from the town's daily newspaper, the *Enterprise Record*. Camusi's father offered to pay the monthly rent.

They commissioned a graphic artist friend and fellow Maltose Falcon member, Chuck Bennett, to develop a design to serve as the company's official logo. They paid $150 for the distinctive picture of a stream–lined meadow set against snow-capped mountains. That same logo design—plus a few tweaks—now adorns every bottle of Sierra Nevada beer.

Grossman and Camusi were still short of cash and equipment, but had ambition and resourcefulness in abundance. Between them (with help from friends), they proceeded to install, in the course of the next eighteen months, a brewhouse, a fermentation cellar, and a bottling line passed down from a soda company.

Buying this equipment brand new would have cost at least $200,000. That kind of money simply wasn't available to the two young entrepreneurs. So when he wasn't building, Grossman hit the road, driving his truck up and down California, Oregon, and Washington, scrounging around defunct dairies for stainless steel pumps and tanks. In this way, he was able to build a brewing kettle by welding an old dairy hopper on top of a recycled stainless steel tank. At a scrap yard in Stockton, he found a cheese vat, brought it back to Chico, and spent weeks hand-drilling thousands of holes in its bottom screen. This would become a mash tun for steeping malted grain and draining residual sugars.

Top left: Bottle filler bought from a soft drink company

Top right: Recycled brewing kettle

Bottom: Hops strainer

He even had a disused pressure cooker delivered from a restaurant in east L.A. Out of necessity, he was gradually developing what became one of the company's trademark mottos: recycle and reuse.

Meanwhile, infrastructure work continued. Grossman and Camusi poured concrete into the building and installed floor drainage. The temptation to cut corners and skimp on expenses was always there, recalls Grossman, but Jack McAuliffe's stern warnings continued to resonate:

"One of the things that McAuliffe had reiterated to us numerous times," Grossman says, "was, 'you've got to do it right, or you're going to have big problems.'" Others were following Anchor's and New Albion's lead and getting into the craft brewing business at the same time, he explains. "They skipped a lot of that difficult infrastructure work, and ended up having lots of problems with hygiene. I was tempted not to do this hard work, but as Jack McCauliffe said, 'Don't bother to get into this business unless you're going to invest in the things that are important.'"

Finally, in November 1980, the ten-barrel brewhouse was ready for production. Grossman and Camusi had decided to experiment with a recipe for a heavy stout, rich in caramel and dry-hopped for extra fragrance. On Saturday morning, November 15, they boiled three hundred pounds of pale malt and roasted barley, and added six pounds of hops. Later that day, they pitched the yeast. The first batch took a week to produce, from the mash-tun stage to bottling. But on November 22, when they pried open the bottles, an unwelcome astringent taste and harsh texture greeted them.

"Simply not good enough for the standards we hope to establish," they decided. They poured the beer down the drain.

They tried another batch, with the same unacceptable results. They switched to a lighter, hoppier recipe, closer to a British bitter. By featuring Cascade hops—a relatively new hop variety from central Oregon—they wanted to impart a distinctive aroma and a spicy, citrus-like flavor to their beer. But the problem of unbalanced taste and texture persisted.

Grossman and Camusi grew concerned: "Over a period of several months, we would do a batch, ferment it, age it, bottle it, taste it, and then decide it wasn't quite right." They conducted extensive analysis in the chemistry labs at Butte College. Was it the quality of malt? Were they using correct temperatures in the fermentation tank? Could it be a lack of micronutrients? Or possibly there was a bacterial growth in their wort?

Once they had ruled out these possibilities, another scenario occurred to them: maybe there was a problem with the yeast culture. The fact is that knowledge of yeast behavior was patchy at best in the early days of craft brewing. It was known that there were two types of yeast: ale yeast (saccharamyces cerevisiae) which was a top-fermenting yeast that floated to the top of the beer and preferred warmer temperatures, and lager yeast (saccharamyces carlsbergensis) that sank to the bottom and required cooler temperatures. Lager was generally more stable because bacteria couldn't propagate as easily in the colder temperatures.

The potential for contamination and spoilage was greater when using ale yeast.

Camusi, in particular, was interested in the problems of yeast management. He wrote letters to leading brewers in Europe and the U.S. asking for their professional input. Some responded promptly with generous advice; others were more guarded with their response.

Yet the inconsistency of their beer continued to puzzle both brewers.

RINGWOOD BREWERY

Telephone 78629
Our ref. PA/ES
Your ref.

Minty's Yard,
New Street,
Ringwood, Hampshire
BH24 3BA

Mr. P. Camusi,
Sierra Nevada Brewing Co.,
2539 Gilman Way
Chico,
California 95926
USA.   24th April 1981.

Dear Mr. Camusi,

Thank you very much for your interesting letter, and I can see exactly what your problem is.

We use in our own brewery a strongly flocculent "Yorkshire" Yeast, which as you say involves rousing the fermentations, but this disadvantage is more than outweighed by the fact that the yeast sediments like lead-shot in bottles or cask. We would happily let you have some if you wish.

A small firm called Micro - Audit are specialists in this field and I enclose their address. I am sure that you will find them helpful.

Always nice to hear from fellow brewers, and realise we all have the same problems in life.

All good wishes.

Yours sincerely,

PETER AUSTIN.

Trying to solve the great yeast mystery: a sample letter in response to Paul Camusi's request for help.

Finally, they contacted a brewer on the East Coast who was familiar with the yeast strain they were using (a strain developed by the Siebel Institute of Technology in Chicago, later to be dubbed "Chico yeast"). His response was beautifully simple: "You need to give it plenty of oxygen." Oxygen poses a dilemma for the homebrewer: use too much and the batch tastes like wet cardboard; use too little, the beer can't breathe and lacks body, robustness and character. Grossman and Camusi had been too conservative in the amount of oxygen they had supplied to their wort to help the yeast get started.

For the next batch, number eleven in the series, they bubbled more oxygen into the wort. After an anxious wait of several days for stabilization and conditioning, they opened up their bottles. The result delighted them. It was crisp and full-bodied, fruity, with a nice balance of hop and malt flavors, a beer they believed the American public might come to love and cherish.

That was in March of 1981. The two entrepreneurs were practically broke after pouring ten precious batches of beer down the drain. Nevertheless, Sierra Nevada Pale Ale was born and ready to go on the market. Within a few years, it would become the best-selling craft beer in American history.

Scenes from the Taproom, Part II
February 26, 2009: Shelter from the Recession

The worst economic crisis in eighty years is sweeping across the globe, toppling banks, wrecking livelihoods, and catapulting well-known companies into bankruptcy. Worldwide, sixty-five million workers lost their jobs in the previous twelve months. In the U.S., an additional 600,000 joined the ranks of the unemployed in the month of January alone. Unemployment figures in the Chico area have reached a fifteen-year high. No one, it seems, is immune from the ravages of the freefall in the global economy. Factories are shut down by the dozen in China. Even the prestigious Japanese automaker, Toyota, has suffered its first operating losses in fifty-nine years, close to $4 billion. Within months, the event has become legendary, known simply as "The Great Crash of 2009."

But the lights still shine in the Taproom and Restaurant at Sierra Nevada Brewing Co. Customers at the bar are doing what they like to do best: sipping the nectar of the gods and chatting freely about the woes and wonders of the world. Remarkably, the craft brewing business remains resilient during the current economic downturn. In fact, the nation's fifteen hundred small breweries continue to track impressive numbers and record sales. Since 2004, according to the American Brewers Association, sales of craft beers have risen a staggering 58 percent. Sierra Nevada continues to record more than $100 million in annual sales.

I've come to the brewery today because Thursdays are cask-conditioned days. I've been told it's a special, not-to-miss occasion for beer lovers. Cask-conditioned beer is a return to the old-fashioned way of serving beer before it was pumped from kegs under carbonated pressure. The beer is naturally carbonated by live yeast in the cask causing ongoing secondary fermentation and enhanced flavors. That's the main reason why loyal devotees sit expectantly in front of the bar this afternoon, awaiting the ceremonial arrival of the barrel (or "firkin" as it's called in certain hallowed circles).

I've arranged to meet Alan Judge here. He and I share much in common. We're both British-born. We both arrived in Chico at the same time in 1988: I joined Chico State; Alan held a series of jobs (at a food co-op, a bakery, a bed and breakfast business, and as a freelance musician) before joining the brewery as jack-of-all trades working in a full range of departments before settling in filtration. We both have a passion for playing and watching soccer (or association football as we used to call it in our childhood days). However, Alan holds an enviable advantage over me: he has a successful professional club that he supports with unswerving loyalty. I have no strong attachment to an English Premier League team as neither my birthplace, Kent, nor my childhood region, Somerset, boast a team of any significance. Alan harbors a fierce passion for his beloved Merseyside clubs, Everton and Liverpool. This gives him bragging rights in our conversation about Britain's national sport. Somehow, it's more authentic to be talking about the mighty Reds of Liverpool rather than my club, Yeovil Town—a third division team whose stadium is within shouting distance of a cow pasture.

But today, I want to talk exclusively about Britain's other national obsession, beer. I have decided that Alan's insights will help me with the story I'm telling about Sierra Nevada Brewing Co.

I sit at the bar waiting for Alan and for the arrival of the cask-conditioned beer when the doors to the brewery are dramatically flung open. A reverential hush falls over the customers at the bar, and there is Alan wheeling in the prized barrel. He wears a smile as wide as the Mersey River. He proceeds to push the barrel of beer down the ramp into the bar area where onlookers pay homage to it with approving nods and whispered words of salutation. It's as if I'm watching the Queen open the Houses of Parliament, her stately procession commanding the respect of loyal subjects on bended knee. Not that Alan ever considered himself belonging to royalty; his working-class roots go deep. But given the dignity and pride he's displaying today, he might as well be wearing the robes of state and bearing the Crown Jewels.

He taps the beer by attaching a hand pump to the barrel. He pulls on the pump several times to skim the foamy head. Then the beer is ready to serve, and he steps aside, his job of delivering the barrel done. He takes a seat next to me.

"How did you pull that stunt off?" I ask incredulously. "I thought you worked in filtration."

"Matt, the cask dude, told me I could do it," he replies in his crisp, Liverpudlian accent. There's fire in his eyes. "Bloody good fun, that."

Alan is of medium height and built with powerful shoulders that capably bear the weight of his ancestors. Unlike me, he has not lost his accent. Mine has become, over the years, a polyglot mix of western drawl and BBC—often mistaken for an Australian twang. Alan still talks a Liverpool patois, called "scouse." Instead of saying "you," scousers prefer "youse." "Howzit?" means "How's it going? "Ay ay!" is the accepted form of greeting.

Nick, the bartender, pours a pint of porter and I'm impressed by its deep brown color with a strong hint of ruby; there is hardly any fizz or foam. I take my first sip and savor the taste of sweet caramel balanced by earthy hop flavors. Phrases from my favorite novelist, Thomas Hardy, come to mind: "full in body, yet brisk as a volcano" was how he described a gravity-poured beer consumed by a character in a cozy Wessex pub at the end of the nineteenth century. The beer, he writes, was "luminous as an autumn sunset and free from streakiness of taste." Yes, it's at times like this when you understand why the craft brewing revolution took off in the first place and why, all around me, there are so many contented customers engaging in joyful and unrestrained banter. Alan introduces me to some colleagues: Abe, a graduate from the Masters Brewer Program at UC Davis and now a brewer; Chris, a recent Chico State graduate who is working his way around various departments; and Rudi, a computer scientist from Nuremberg, Germany, who is here on a two-month assignment to review the brewery's computer and automation systems.

They decide to give me an education about the technical aspects of beer production. With my limited technical vocabulary I'm able to stay in the conversation for several minutes but they soon confound me with phrases like "racking to secondary," "batch sparging," and "centrifugation." Inevitably, the word "flocculation" comes up again and I'm still unaware of its true meaning. I begin to feel out of my depth so I try to change the subject, to get them talking about working conditions at the brewery, especially now that it operates on a 24–7 schedule. Then Alan says something that will stick with me for some time: "You develop camaraderie akin to being at sea, on a ship," he says. "Like Shackleton on the *Endurance*. Wacky hours, sleep deprivation, and when you reach land, it's party time."

Wait a minute! Did he say Shackleton of the *Endurance*?

At school in England, I learned all about Sir Ernest Shackleton and his aborted expedition to the South Pole in 1914. Along with Scott of the Antarctic, he was deemed a shining example of the type of failed British hero who was guaranteed to stoke imperial pride and ambition for generations to come. Shackleton's ship, the *Endurance,* was crushed by pack ice, forcing the fearless captain to guide his crew on foot across eight hundred miles of drifting ice packs to eventual safety, one of the greatest survival stories in the history of human exploration. Not a single life was lost, and most of the credit was given to the wise and compassionate leadership of Shackleton. All very inspiring.

But what's this got to do with working at a brewery located in the upper central valley of northern California? At first, I'm puzzled.

Then I recall an image of Shackleton from my schoolboy history text—the wizened beard, the high forehead, the compassionate smile—and at that moment I have a sort of beer-induced epiphany. Suddenly, it all makes sense. What Alan is trying to tell me is that Ken Grossman, Sierra Nevada's talismanic owner, is a modern-day Shackleton caring for his shipmates while a cruel Antarctic storm rages all around. After all, the working conditions at the brewery are legendary: the wellness program, the free massage therapy, not to mention the monthly allowance of free beer.

But I don't press this thought further, not for now at least.

It's time for another round of beer.

Alan drains his glass, and then stops in his tracks. "Bloody hell," he exclaims. "I must be seeing a ghost. Look who's here." A white-bearded man with a Jerry Garcia smile has suddenly appeared, standing next to our group. "This man is a god around these parts," Alan says with the conviction of an evangelist. "A god, I tell you."

I'm wondering if it could be the legendary Fritz Maytag of Anchor Brewing Company, or Jack McAuliffe, the guru of New Albion Brewing Company, both venerated members of the craft brewing profession. I've read extensively about their legacies but have never seen them in person. Plus, my second pint of porter is beginning to assert itself and the thin line that separates fantasy from reality is starting to blur. It turns out he's Rob Atkinson, a popular bartender in the 1990s and one of the original workers at Sierra Nevada Brewing Co. when it was operating in a small warehouse on the outskirts of town. He has not been seen around these parts in a long time. He seems perfectly content to just drink and listen to our group's lively banter. But when he does speak, he is soft spoken and I can't hear him very well. There's an air of mystery to the man so I take Alan aside and inquire further.

"Suffice to say, being the barman for years, a lot of water went under his bridge," he says cryptically. Fair enough. Some things are obviously better left alone. It makes me realize yet again that I am an outsider writing this story and that, as such, I must respect certain trade secrets that are strictly off-limits.

By dinnertime, a *Who's Who* of Sierra Nevada key players has made an appearance at the Taproom. Ken Grossman greets well-wishers with grace and charm, looking and acting every inch like an Ernest Shackleton. The head brewer, Steve Dresler, holds court with a captive audience. There are others that I will come to know later in the course of researching the book: Terence Sullivan, Bill Manley, Rob Fraser, Scott Jennings, Cheri Chastain, and Jim Mellem. I'm not sure but I think I also spot Ken Grossman's two children, Brian and Sierra, who have recently assumed important administrative positions at the brewery. Good cheer flows freely through the Taproom and adjoining Restaurant on this crisp winter's afternoon in northern California.

Before I depart, I have one more question for Alan. It's a question that I have put to many experts in recent months: *Is the craft-brewing industry recession proof?*

Alan fixes me with an incredulous stare as if to say, "Are you daft, mate?" Then he points to the scrum of customers lining the bar: "Look at these people," he says. "They're here to enjoy good beer and good times. If anything, this is where you come for some recession medicine."

Given the pleasant buzz ringing in my head and the high spirits swirling around me, I'm not about to disagree. I wobble out of the brewery, all smiles and fully fortified.

CHAPTER THREE

From Fledgling Microbrewery to Flagship Craft Brewery 1981–1999

EARLY MARKETING AND DISTRIBUTION IN CHICO

IN MARCH 1981, Sierra Nevada Pale Ale went on the market in Chico.

Three decades later, it's easy to forget how radically different this style of beer was regarded at the time. It has since gone on to become one of the most celebrated success stories of the craft-brewing movement and remains the company's best-selling beer, accounting for over 85 percent of its total volume output. (Sierra Nevada Pale Ale posted more than $81 million in sales for 2009, according to figures by Information Resources Inc., Chicago). It is one of the benchmarks by which other craft beers continue to be judged. The difference in taste appreciation between then and now illustrates how far consumer sophistication has developed in the past thirty years, thanks in good measure to breweries like Sierra Nevada.

Yet, in the early 1980s, Sierra Nevada Pale Ale was seen as a fringe beer that broke from American brewing orthodoxy on many fronts: it had a high count of bitterness units (38 as opposed to an average of 10–15 in an industrial beer), boasted high alcohol content (5.6% as opposed to the 4% range for commercial brews), and used two-row American pale malt as opposed to six-row (the six-row variety was easier to use with cereal adjuncts such as corn and rice because of its higher protein content and was therefore favored by big beer companies). Another distinguishing characteristic of the beer was its unusually heavy hop flavor and robust aroma. Grossman and Camusi were among the first commercial brewers to feature whole-cone, U.S. grown Cluster and Cascade hops for flavoring and aroma. Choosing Cascade hops, in particular, proved to be an important watershed moment in American beer history. One beer commentator, Don Russell, writes: "In an era when American beer drinkers might've found Becks and Heineken a flavor challenge, the use of Cascades in Sierra Nevada Pale Ale was a balls-out statement of beer-making machismo." That's because Cascades had a distinctive style; they smothered the nose with what Russell calls "a fresh wallop of citrus and freshly cut grass." He claims that "it wouldn't be an overstatement to suggest that the single most important ingredient in the entire modern American beer renaissance is Cascade hops."

Additionally, the beer was bottle-conditioned. This meant that a small amount of yeast was added to the beer in the bottle, resulting in secondary fermentation and the release of natural carbonation. Until 1984, the beer was unfiltered so that volatile flavors and compounds typically featured in the beer. In fact, you never quite knew what you were getting when you opened a bottle of Pale Ale: perhaps it might pour a little cloudy or foamy or perhaps it would be yeasty, even slightly sulfuric in taste and texture.

Curiously, it was these surprises that increased the beer's mystique. Its deep amber color, fragrant aroma, bright citrusy flavor, and robust malty presence made Sierra Nevada Pale Ale something unique to savor. "I don't know who in Chico is making this stuff," gushed the food critic of the *San Francisco Chronicle,* "but

I want to give them a gold medal." Within a year, the beer had won the Grand Prize at the 1982 Great American Beer Festival in Boulder, Colorado.

Looking back at this moment in history, beer connoisseur Charlie Papazian writes: "It was the dawn of what was to become

Ken Grossman and Paul Camusi

Ken Grossman and bottling machine

the most popular style of microbrewed craft beer, American pale ale, and the Sierra Nevada Brewing Company of Chico, California, pioneered the way (11)."

Grossman and Camusi had a product they believed in yet no marketing strategy, nor even a systematic method of working shifts. Between them, they brewed, bottled, and distributed—assigning labor and responsibilities on an ad hoc basis.

They had a 3,000-square-foot warehouse crammed with hand-built and cast-off equipment. They used a '57 Chevy for transporting beer about town and picking up supplies from the Bay Area. They often worked from 5:00 in the morning until 8:00 at night. They couldn't afford to sell the beer in 6-packs so they distributed it to retailers in 24-bottle cases. In turn, the retailers would sell single bottles for 85 cents. Grossman and Camusi used long-necked bottles bought from commercial breweries which then had to be washed out one by one; the original labels had to be thoroughly scrubbed and peeled away, which proved to be time-intensive and laborious. In between brewing and bottling, they walked the streets of downtown Chico, from door to door, around the bars, restaurants, and liquor stores, selling one case at a time, then returning later to pick up the empty bottles for reuse.

Pale Ale soon found a particularly appreciative market at the local student bars—La Salles, Madison Bear, and a hangout called Canal Street (no longer around). In their first year, Sierra Nevada sold the equivalent of five hundred barrels of Pale Ale, exclusively in the city of Chico. Not bad, the brewers thought, especially as they had no official marketing plan or advertising strategy. The beer's popularity was spreading exclusively by word of mouth.

But they were ambitious to sell beyond Chico. In early 1982, they signed on their first full-time employee, Steve Harrison, a childhood friend of Grossman's also hailing from Woodland Hills. Harrison's main responsibility was to deliver beer to bars and res-

Steve Harrison, first full-time employee at Sierra Nevada

taurants and fill in at the brewery, as needed. His other responsibility was to make contact with distributors in order to secure
some kind of market niche. Up to this point, the company had
self-distributed its beer following the model adopted by Maytag
and McAuliffe.

In the 1980s, the beer industry was organized into a three-
tier system as a result of post-Prohibition restructuring: first, the
breweries (who produced the beer); second, the distributors or
wholesalers (who shipped the beer to markets around the country); and finally, the retailers (who sold the beer to consumers).
Distributors thus carried considerable influence: without their
cooperation, a company had limited marketing opportunities.
At the time, they were mainly interested in servicing well-es-
tablished brewing companies and did not provide marketing or
sales support for upstarts. A company like Sierra Nevada, with no
brand profile as yet, found it difficult to break into a retail market
monopolized by big American industrial breweries and a handful
of imports. Other microbreweries in Novato (DeBakker Brewing Company) and Boulder (Boulder Brewing Company) were
facing similar problems. Even Jack McAuliffe's New Albion was
struggling to maintain its early momentum because it could not
break into a wider market beyond northern California. Eventually, McAuliffe would be forced to close his brewery in 1982. These
companies needed no reminding of the stark reality that, in the
United States, six breweries still produced over 90 percent of the
nation's beer and maintained a virtual monopoly on the distribution business.

Charlie Papazian put his finger on the problem: "Great beer
was being microbrewed, but the system failed to provide beer
drinkers the access to beers they were growing to love" (28). Because of consolidation in the early '80s, beverage distribution was
an industry run by a small number of big companies using bigger
warehouses, bigger shipping fleets, and covering larger areas. Un-
fortunately, this also meant that you had to be a bigger company

to attract their attention.

Despite this handicap, Sierra Nevada's popularity in Chico—as well as their sales figures—continued to grow. Meeting the increased demand meant Grossman and Camusi soon had to double production capacity. Their brewery would need a serious upgrade to keep up with demand. They also heard that in Germany, breweries were closing at the rate of about one a week and could be purchased at bargain prices. Whereas American microbreweries were multiplying in number and expanding in size, in Germany the consolidation of national breweries such as Becks and Sternburg had, by the early 1980s, squeezed out many mid-sized, regional breweries. It would be cheaper for Grossman and Camusi to fly out to Germany and purchase a defunct brewery rather than try to build one from scratch at home. As an added incentive, they would have the opportunity to acquire equipment distinguished by centuries of beer-making tradition.

BAVARIAN INTERLUDE

I N LATE 1982, they went over to Germany. For Grossman and Camusi, visiting Germany was almost a rite of initiation. They admired the wide variety of available beer styles (from the malt-based "altbier" of the north to the "hefeweizen" wheat beer of the south); they marveled at the 1516 Beer Purity Law (Reinheitsgebot), which forbade the use of any ingredients other than malt, hops, and water (later yeast) in the brewing process; above all, they were thrilled at the opportunity to purchase valuable equipment so inexpensively.

They had been told that in a town called Aschaffenburg, twenty-five miles southeast of Frankfurt, there was a Bavarian brewery (Bavaria-Brauerei) up for sale. Aschaffenburg was roughly the same size of Chico with a population of approximately 60,000. Like Chico, it had garnered many awards for its quality of life, voted by *Stern* magazine as the best place to live in Germany on several occasions. Located in a northwest corner of Bavaria (formerly, Franconia), it boasted the distinction of having more breweries per square mile than anywhere else in Germany. Fortunately for Grossman and Camusi, one of these was up for sale and the two Californians were given preference for its possible purchase. Inside the brewhouse, they were shown two vessels both made of brightly polished copper, standing side by side like proud sisters: a lauter tun used for separating sweet wort from spent malt, and a brew-kettle where hops are added to the wort and then boiled together for up to two hours. Both vessels had been hammered into shape by expert craftsmen, starting at ground level with a wide circular base then curving elegantly into a narrow swan-like neck that reached into the ceiling. The total capacity for the brewery was one hundred barrels.

Grossman and Camusi visualized these vessels as the heart and soul of an expanded Sierra Nevada Brewing Co. They negotiated with a representative from Huppmann, the parent company that owned the brewing vessels, and paid $20,000 for the equipment.

A thing of beauty—the Huppmann brewing vessels

Removing the Huppmann kettles from the Aschaffenburg brewery

Each manufacturing company has a distinctive design style for its brewhouse equipment: Huppmann, located in the Bavarian town of Kitzingen, was particularly famous for its sleek, elegant, burnished copper vessels. It was an aesthetic that agreed with the Chico pair.

Buying the brewery was the easy part. Transporting the equipment back to California was another matter. It cost a further $20,000 to have the vessels removed from the building and packed into wooden crates. As the owner watched the dismantling operation, he chuckled and said to Grossman: "I don't think these will ever be installed again." A few months—and another $20,000 worth of shipping costs—later, Grossman and Camusi picked up the two crates at Oakland docks, transferring them to two flatbed trailers that they had hired for the day. The crates were considerably wider than the trucks, however, and this resulted in a perilous 200-mile journey up the Sacramento Valley. Back in Chico, they did not know what to do with the newly-

A few weeks later, the crated Huppmann kettles arrive in Chico

acquired equipment as the vessels were certainly too large to fit into the Gilman Way building.

Finding and paying for a new brewhouse would be prohibitively expensive, nearly $2 million by one estimate. They met with various venture funding groups but most would not touch the fledgling company. The one exception was a distributor in northern California that owned Calistoga Water Company. However, there was a catch: he wanted to own 51 percent of the company in return. This was not the first or last time that Sierra Nevada Brewing Co. received handsome buyout offers from speculators. Nor would it be the last time that Grossman, in particular, refused to yield independence and control of a company that he had invested so much of his life in.

Grudgingly, Grossman and Camusi decided to postpone rebuilding the German brewery equipment. It would have to sit in storage, boxed up in crates, for a few more years. In the meantime, they continued to expand Gilman Way. The dream of becoming a midsized European-style brewery was put on hold; they realized they would have to continue operating as a fledgling company.

Gilman Way was originally designed for an annual output of 1,500 barrels. But by late 1983, the demand for Sierra Nevada beers had reached the point where the company needed to significantly boost production. They added tanks and more machinery then took over an adjacent building and installed a more efficient bottling line acquired from Fritz Maytag. Their main goal at this point was to produce more beer from the old plant.

Financing continued to be a worrisome problem. Even though they had been demonstrably frugal, the $60,000 spent on bringing the German brewery to Chico would need to be repaid sooner or later.

BOHEMIAN RHAPSODY

BY THIS time, they had hired two new workers, Bob August and Steve Dresler. When the Huppmann crates arrived in Chico after their transatlantic shipment, a photograph of the two new workers standing alongside Camusi and Grossman was taken by Steve Harrison. The group came to be known around the brewery as "The Fab Four." In truth, the four of them more resemble outlaws from a Clint Eastwood western than the mop-haired pop stars from Liverpool. None more so than Steve Dresler, a tall man with shoulder-length blonde hair, large eyeglass frames, and the demeanor of an amiable Viking.

Dresler had recently graduated from Chico State with a double major in biology and chemistry. His first job in Chico was conducting corrosion control on the metal coating of aircraft for Aero Union Company, a firefighting unit, at the town's airport. He had been a homebrewer on the side and worked part-time at The Home Brew Shop which now had new owners. Word reached him that the new brewery in town was hiring part-time workers. The pay would be half his Aero Union wage and he would have to give up his full-time work. Nevertheless, he grabbed the opportunity. "This was back in my organic, hippy days," he recalls wistfully. He resigned from Aero Union and took the job. "So I came in and worked packing on the bottling line, spent part of that afternoon with Ken, after we'd done bottling, and we had some beers and a chat." You're hired, Grossman said. He worked part-time for a few months. "Then I got a chance to brew on a Saturday and got a foot in the door at the brewhouse." Before long he was hired full-time, at thirty to thirty-five hours a week, $5 an hour. That was in 1983.

Looking back, Dresler marvels: "Nobody at that time envisioned anything like where we are today but you know, we were a very eclectic group of people, very passionate about what we were doing, into having fun, very creative individuals, people that were able to think on their feet and work things through."

This spirit is captured in another photograph taken a few months later, after several more hires had been made. The photograph sits on Ken Grossman's desk to this day as a reminder, perhaps, of those early days of buoyant innocence. It should be

The Fab Four: Bob August, Ken Grossman, Paul Camusi, Steve Dresler

titled "Bohemian Rhapsody" for it seems to capture the zeitgeist of this particular moment in brewing history: the swaggering, bohemian, bright-eyed idealism that animated these Young Turks. There's Grant Boswell (now a nurse living in Bend, Oregon), Ken Grossman, Frank Comanday, Bob August, Steve Philpott (now a teacher living in Sacramento). They all look at the camera with an in-your-face chutzpah; all, that is, except for Boswell who smiles enigmatically at his peers as if he's unsure whether to be amused or embarrassed by their audacious antics. Grossman and Philpott cockily swig from bottles of beer; Grossman looks bodacious yet relaxed, Philpott is shirtless and without shame.

This was the face of the microbrewing movement in the early 1980s. The loose dress code—bare chests, shorts, sandals, overalls, rubber boots—says it all.

How comfortable they look with their newfound notoriety—like surfers riding the mystic wave. They're in the zone, and they know it. Even though they can't be certain how far or

Bohemian Rhapsody. Grant Boswell, Ken Grossman, Frank Comanday, Bob August, Steve Philpott.

how fast this wave will carry them, they don't seem to worry or care.

Later that year, they hired Ed McLaughlin, one of Grossman's friends from his days of working at Chico Bike. McLaughlin helped out with brewing, but stayed with the company for less than a year before moving on to start a string of bike businesses around Chico and in Europe.

They became bolder with their choice of beer styles. In 1983, they started Bigfoot, a name suggested by one of Grossman's camping buddies in honor of a local legend from Mount Shasta, 140 miles north of Chico. It's a barley wine with very strong alcohol content, 9.6 percent ABV, but also robust with hops and malt.

Earlier, during his annual hop pilgrimage to Yakima, Grossman found exceptionally good-quality Cascades with strong aromatics. He decided to celebrate with a big-hopped IPA (India pale ale) yet with full malt body in anticipation of the coming of winter and its seasonal festivities. This was to become the much-vaunted Celebration Ale—still a highly anticipated seasonal, available from mid-October through springtime.

They were still operating according to semi-anarchic principles: brewing, filtering, and bottling with no clear division of labor. They followed a simple work schedule: Monday, Wednesday, and Friday were brewing days; Tuesday and Thursday were bottling and packaging days. Whenever necessary, they worked over the weekends. But by mid-1984, this was no longer a viable model. Sierra Nevada had outgrown its "all hands on deck" approach to brewing. Like it or not, a new managerial structure was needed.

Charlie Papazian describes the dilemma Sierra Nevada faced after he visited the Gilman Way brewery in the mid-'80s. "In the beginning," he writes, "the maximum they could brew was thirty barrels a week. At the time this seemed like a gold mine, but the reality of maintaining beer quality, the increasing costs of packaging and selling beer and keeping and paying their employees well and the need to make a profit in order to reinvest in their growing business became evident as the demand for their beer increased (13)".

For the first time, specific job assignments were made: Dresler was placed in charge of brewing, Bob August handled packaging and filtration, Steve Harrison was given sales and distribution, and Ken Grossman took overall managerial command. Still, the way Dresler recalls it, the assignment process was rather haphazard: "So all of a sudden I'm the brewmaster," he tells me with a grin. "Basically, we were going to get our own business cards so Ken said, 'what do you want yours to say?'" Clearly, the company was not about to sacrifice its solidly bohemian principles overnight.

The one key player not involved in the restructuring was Paul Camusi who seemed to be withdrawing more and more from

Bohemian Rhapsody reprise. Paul Camusi, Delana Camusi, Rob Atkinson, Brian Haley, Richmond Talbot, Steve Harrison, Steve Dresler, Bob August, Ken Grossman.

Bob August, filtration   Steve Dresler, brewmaster

brewing operations, and this was something that everyone at Gil-man Way started to notice.

KEY ENDORSEMENTS
(AND PRODUCT PLACEMENT)

A T LAST, the company was able to penetrate markets be-yond the Chico catchment area. Sophisticated beer drinkers from all around the country were starting to realize it was no accident that Pale Ale had been awarded Grand Prize by the Great American Beer Festival in 1982. "How can we get this stuff to our home town?" they asked. A series of oppor-tune endorsements helped to consolidate Sierra Nevada's reputa-tion, catapulting their sales, and catching the eye of national dis-tributors such as Consumers Distributing and A&D Distributors.

The first endorsement came from Alice Waters, owner of famed Berkeley restaurant Chez Panisse, who started serving Pale Ale at her restaurant in the early '80s. Since opening its doors in 1971, Chez Panisse had dedicated itself to taste, consistency, en-vironmental stewardship, and the sustenance of local traditions—values shared equally by Grossman and Camusi. Adopting Sierra Nevada beer was, Waters said, consistent with her philosophy of serving only the highest quality products in order to afford the most satisfying dining experience. "The Chez Panisse endorse-ment was great," recalls Grossman. "It gave us exposure to foodies and other restaurateurs. Alice was doing innovative things with food. So that was positive for building our brand." Just as Alice Waters recreated the tastes and flavors of food she had enjoyed as an exchange student in France, Grossman and Camusi were attempting to revive brewing tastes and traditions from the Old World.

Brand building by free advertising via endorsements and word of mouth: this was to become the Sierra Nevada credo. The unofficial company policy on advertising remains to this day, "our advertising comes out of a 12-ounce bottle." Sierra Nevada continues to avoid advertising in mainstream media (although it does place advertisements in trade journals).

Meanwhile, a further series of influential endorsements followed on from Alice Waters' promotion. Jerry Garcia, talismanic leader of the cult band, Grateful Dead, revealed that Sierra Nevada Porter was his favorite beer. After that, Sierra Nevada beer was always served at Grateful Dead concerts, becoming the beer of choice for most Deadheads. In 1983, Stan Sesser wrote an article in the *San Francisco Chronicle* in which he described Sierra Nevada Celebration Ale as the "best beer ever made in America."

The Chico brewery was quickly building a cult following.

Then they got a big break from happy coincidence and luck. The father of a Chico State student was the statewide head beverage buyer for a large supermarket chain. Whenever he visited Chico to visit his daughter, he would try out a new brew. Says Grossman, "He thought what we were doing on Gilman Way was quaint, he wanted to help us, so we started getting some feature advertisements for free." Across the state, now it was not unusual to see Sierra Nevada Pale Ale and Porter and two newly created seasonals, a winter Celebration and a Summerfest, alongside imports such as Guinness, Bass, and Heineken in grocery stores.

On May 25, 1986, a featured article in the Sunday color supplement magazine of the *San Francisco Examiner* offered an exclusive profile of the Chico company. Written by Michael Castleman, it was entitled "The Beer That's Making Chico Famous" and displayed a lead photograph of Camusi and Grossman, dressed casually in Sierra Nevada t-shirts and jeans, sitting on stacked cases of beer in a field of tall grass; a bank of puffy white clouds against an expansive blue sky serves as a scenic backdrop. They are smiling confidently and saluting the photographer with glasses of beer. The article chronicles their rags to riches story with obvious admiration. Beer connoisseurs, observes Castleman, "have used such superlatives, it's as though Moses brought a few cases down from Mount Sinai." And he notes that the adulation is no longer restricted to the West Coast. "Bars, liquor stores, and distributors from the Bay Area to Connecticut—even guys off the street—were screaming for Sierra Nevada beer."

Another important boost came from the national exposure increasingly given to Sierra Nevada by popular media such as TV and movies. In the following two decades, it would not be unusual to spot the distinctive green label of Sierra Nevada Pale Ale bottles in the hit comedy series *Friends*—on top of Joey and Chandler's refrigerator amongst an assortment of leading craft brews. Or the beer would feature in a Judd Apatow movie; for example, there's a prominent scene in *Knocked Up* (2007) where two protagonists discuss the pitfalls of marriage over conspicuously-placed bottles of Sierra Nevada Pale Ale. Even though the brewery pays a modest annual fee to a Hollywood placement company (whose job is to secure screen time for the product they represent), many times Sierra Nevada is used simply because the director or producer enjoys the beer so much and requests to have it on the set. Says Steve Grossman, ambassador for the company's public relations: "They just happen to like our beer. We don't seek out their endorsements."

THE STORY of Chau Tien Pale Ale, dubbed as "the first Asian beer made in the U.S.," illustrates the extent to which Sierra Nevada Brewing Co. was proving to be an inspiration for upstart entrepreneurs. During the summer of 1985, Tony Nguyen, a successful electrical engineer from the Bay Area, had a dream about a dragon and angel that encouraged him to leave his job and take up brewing. In the early days of his engineering apprenticeship, he had drunk Sierra Nevada Pale Ale, and this was the flavor and style that he now wanted to emulate. Between 1985 and 1987, he visited Chico several times, took notes, and

Front cover of The San Francisco Examiner, *May 25, 1986*

met with Grossman, Dresler, and others. Determined to fulfill his dream of becoming "Tuan, the Beer Guy," he brewed under contract at Anderson Valley Brewery Co. in Mendocino County where Chau Tien Pale Ale—modeled on Sierra Nevada Pale Ale—continues to be brewed and still proves particularly popular in Vietnamese restaurants in the Bay Area.

Sierra Nevada was now growing at just under 50 percent a year. In just five years, they had gone from producing 500 barrels to 12,000. And they were distributing to seven states, predominantly in the West. The ten workers were working around the clock, six-and-a-half days a week. It was no longer a hobby or labor of love or semi-amateurish operation. This was big business. Says Grossman: "Finally, we got to the point where we were beginning to turn customers away so there was more and more pressure on us to do something."

The microbrewing industry was at a crossroads. The mid '80s were heady times—as recalled by Papazian: "These were adventurous times when doctors, airline pilots, computer programmers, lawyers, teachers, social workers, salespeople and many other professionals were giving up their jobs, risking it all to pursue their passion for beer" (27). He continues: "... everyone felt the excitement of being a pioneer on the frontier of a movement that was sure to win over the beer enthusiast who savored the flavor of real beer" (27).

By 1986, a new phrase, "craft brewery," was gaining popularity in brewing circles to describe a company that used traditional methods for producing beer. An arbitrary figure of 10,000 barrels was used to define the difference between a microbrewery and a craft brewery (the cut-off figure was quickly raised to 15,000 barrels). Sierra Nevada was now close to that symbolic threshold. It would soon cross over and become, technically speaking, a craft brewery. As Sierra Nevada entered its adolescence, two challenges emerged that would cause considerable tension throughout the late '80s and through much of the '90s:

the first was relocating and expanding the brewery and the second was the buyout of cofounder, Paul Camusi, who had become less interested in the business now that it was growing out of its fledgling phase.

MOVE TO 20th STREET

F OR NOW, at least, the two business partners continued to work together on necessary expansion plans. In 1987, they struck a deal with a local speculator and builder, Lou Chrysler, allowing them to build a new brewery on a lot strategically located close to Highway 99, a major artery running north-south along the Sacramento Valley. This would become the site of the current brewery located at 1075 East 20th Street. Chrysler had acquired fifteen acres with the intention of dividing the parcel of land into smaller lots. He was happy to build a physical structure for the brewery on one of them and then lease it out to the company with a future option to buy. This arrangement meant that Grossman and Camusi only needed to pay for equipment and infrastructure inside the new building. They secured loans from Bank of America and from Paul Camusi's mother, and then hired a local architect, Ed Hoiland, to design a 25,000 square foot brewery alongside a 2,700 square foot pub.

Chrysler agreed to build the shell of the brewery according to blueprints drawn up by Hoiland. The idea was to keep the

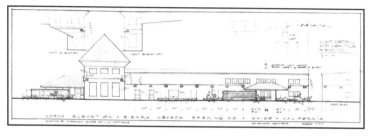

Blueprint for the original brewery. Courtesy of Ed Hoiland, architect.

building's dimensions as close as possible to the Aschaffenburg brauerei from where the copper kettles had originated. Grossman and Camusi wanted their brewery to have a distinctly Bavarian appearance mixed with California colors and complexion. The result was an attractive building that perfectly expressed the company's defining ethos: assertive yet not aggressive, bold yet not showy, proud yet not vain. Its centerpiece was the brewing hall housing the copper kettles: a sandstone building with floor-to-ceiling windows topped by a steeply-pitched roof whose tiles were painted electric blue.

While the brewery was being built, Grossman got on with the business of fabricating, welding, assembling, and fitting on the opposite side of the street where he leased a building owned at the time by Royal Crown Bottling Company. He had bought a vintage 1962 Semco bottle filler from an equipment dealer, capable of filling four hundred bottles a minute. His intention was to rebuild it from scratch, then transfer it ready-made into the new site. "We built every piece ourselves," says Grossman. "Now,

Construction of the 20th Street brewery begins

After five years in crates, the Huppmann kettles are finally released from captivity

in hindsight, that was a stupid thing. It was a tremendously long, laborious process."

Next, it was the turn of the Huppmann kettles which had been stored away in crates for five years. The only problem was that even though Grossman had been on hand to witness the dismantling of the kettles in Germany, he was not sure if he could remember how to put them back together again. In fact, the German brewery owner had laughed behind Grossman's back at the idea that they would ever be reassembled. Grossman recalls: "He was sure that the kettles would never be put together again. He said something in German to the guys I'd hired to help me take it out. He said, 'This is going to be scrap.'" So Grossman consulted Fritz Pfister, the Huppmann technician who had supervised the dismantling. With the help of a local engineer, Boyd Buck, Grossman pieced together the kettles over several months of trial-by-error labor. At the end of it all, Pfister came to appreciate Grossman's mechanical genius, not to mention his refusal to give up on what appeared initially to be a seemingly intractable problem. Pfister and Grossman have stayed loyal friends ever since.

On November 15, 1987, the new 100-barrel brewhouse opened for business, featuring the shiny copper kettles, four open-tank fermenters, and eleven 68-barrel secondary fermenters. Grossman and Camusi had designed the brewhouse for an annual output capacity of 60,000 barrels, even though they doubted whether they could ever hit this target.

By coincidence, November 15 was also Sierra Nevada's seventh anniversary so the company decided to celebrate in style. Grossman admits this was "a bad idea. We were trying to have a party while brewing our first batch. A bunch of stuff didn't work. We ended up with a foot and a half of water in the basement, in the middle of our party. What was supposed to be fun ended up being a mucky mess."

Despite the initial setback, there was an immediate jump in production. Says brewmaster Dresler: "All of a sudden, you're

Fermentation tanks are installed

not doing 15-barrel batches anymore. You're doing 100 barrels. We were all putting in brutally long days. I think at one point I put in twenty or thirty days straight. Yet it was the best of times."

Sierra Nevada started to enjoy phenomenal growth. Grossman comments: "It's not as if we had to sell our souls to grow. We just rode the wave up. We were growing well ahead of our peers." Adds Dresler: "We were starting to come into the higher echelons. We were successful. We were highly regarded within the brewing community."

In 1991, Steve Harrison, Sierra Nevada's sales and marketing director, struck a deal with Tom Potter of the Craft Brewers Guild of Brooklyn, New York, guaranteeing distribution rights to the important East Coast market. "Sierra quickly became our best-selling beer, after Brooklyn Brewery products," writes Tom Potter in his book *Beer School* (2005). He continues: "Its Pale Ale became something of a phenomenon in New York. ... We sold it with terrific enthusiasm" (98-99).

They were riding a wave—no longer just a fledgling microbrewery but rather a craft brewery with flagship status around the nation.

CRAFT BREW BUBBLE

THE EARLY 1990s were a euphoric time for the micro and craft brewing industry, led by Sierra Nevada Brewing Co. By 1993, Sierra Nevada's annual production was pushing well beyond the 60,000-barrel mark; a few years earlier, Grossman and Camusi would have considered this number a fanciful pipe dream. They started brewing around the clock, putting in 24-hour shifts, 362 or 363 days a year, taking only Christmas and Thanksgiving Day off. A series of upgrades followed, with the addition of another mash tun, receiver vessel, unitanks, and secondary fermenters. They could now do as many as eight brews a day. By 1995, they were up to 201,000 barrels and stretched to full capacity.

All around the country, startup breweries were experiencing astonishing success and rapid growth. Some took this opportune moment to explore riskier, market-driven methods of raising capital and turning profits. In August 1995, Redhook Ale Brewery (Seattle, Washington) went public with an initial public offering (IPO) of $17 a share that increased to $27 a share at the end of the first day of trading. Redhook netted $46 million from its IPO and saw an immediate dramatic increase in its sales and profits. Additionally, Redhook had, the previous year, sold 25 percent of its ownership to Anheuser-Busch in order to gain access to A-B's extensive distribution network. Clearly, a new business model was proving attractive to some entrepreneurs in the brewing business. (By the time the craft beer bubble burst, Redhook traded for as low as $2 a share and was barely able to survive as a viable business. Currently, it is publicly traded as part of the Craft Brewers Alliance along with Widmer Brothers, Goose Island Brewing Company, and Kona Brewing Company).

The most successful and conspicuous follower of the Wall Street model was Jim Koch of Boston Beer Company. A graduate of Harvard Law School, Koch started out as a consultant for Boston Consulting Group, but then decided to try his hand at craft brewing, following in his family's brewing footsteps. His business strategy differed from the usual craft-brew model on several counts: first, he promoted lager rather than ale as his company's flagship beer; second, he adopted contract brewing as a means of farming out his brewing operation to other breweries, thus allowing him to focus his energies on advertising and marketing; third, in 1995, Boston Beer Company went public, with an initial public offering of over five million shares valued at $20 a share (by 2010, the value had climbed to $70 a share).

More than once, Grossman was approached by big breweries. But he was determined to hold out as an independently owned company. There was another threat on the horizon. Big brewers were trying to capture the craft beer market—even though, at less than 5 percent, it was still relatively small compared to the overall beer market. In 1996, Anheuser-Busch released a beer called Pacific Ridge Pale Ale and promoted it heavily in northern California. I remember seeing advertisements for the beer on billboards around town. "Why on earth would anyone want to promote such a beer in a town where Sierra Nevada Pale Ale is king?" I wondered. Clearly, Anheuser-Busch felt that if Pacific Ridge could make inroads in Chico, then it would most likely take off in other parts of the country where Sierra Nevada was favored. Pacific Ridge Pale Ale was practically a clone of Sierra Nevada Pale Ale: the bottle label had similar yellow and green motifs while the beer had a similar copper appearance and the same citrusy flavor profile. By undercutting the cost of Sierra Nevada Pale Ale by almost a dollar, Anheuser-Busch hoped to win over bargain hunters. But the strategy failed. Discerning consumers could clearly tell the difference between the two beers. Within a year, Pacific Ridge Pale Ale disappeared altogether from the supermarket shelves.

Sierra Nevada's most pressing challenge remained meeting demand. The company continued to initiate significant upgrades to its Chico plant. In February 1996, a state-of-the-art bottling line was installed, costing $2 million. Not only was it quicker (at 650 bottles per minute) but it also spilled less beer and, perhaps most importantly, it was allowing less oxygen to seep into the beer thereby damaging its quality. Remarkably, only two days of brewing production were lost during the radical changeover: the old line was dismantled and removed on a Sunday; by the following Wednesday afternoon, the new line was churning out its first bottles.

It was clear that another wholesale expansion of the brewery was urgently required. The company was brewing 363 days a year, around the clock, yet still struggled to meet customer demand. Therefore, the decision was made to build another brewhouse— a replica of the original, only twice the size. It would be situated next door to the original brewhouse.

In late 1997, Grossman and a team of technical advisers flew out to Germany again, revisiting the Huppmann headquarters in Kitzingen. This time, they were not looking to buy a defunct brewery. Now, they knew what they wanted from the outset: a brand new 200-barrel brewhouse complete with the latest equip-

Construction of the West Brewhouse

ment offerings in filtration, refrigeration, and cellaring; most importantly, they wanted to acquire two copper kettles to match the originals they had purchased in Aschaffenburg sixteen years earlier.

Brewing technology had advanced significantly in the two decades between Grossman's visits to Germany: machines were

Assembly of the new Huppmann kettles

now more dependent on automation; cleaning procedures were performed by sophisticated cleaning-in-place (CIP) procedures rather than by hand. As a result, brewing kettles were more commonly made out of stainless steel instead of copper, as in the past. But Grossman wanted his new kettles to have a copper exterior so that their external appearance matched the originals. A compromise was reached that allowed Grossman to take advantage of new technology while maintaining loyalty to traditional craftsmanship: the kettles would be lined with stainless steel on the inside but, on the outside, they would retain their distinctive copper character. With the help of his friend Fritz Pfister, Huppmann's systems engineer, he commissioned the same German coppersmiths who had worked on the originals to hammer out the new kettles. Indeed, they were brought out of retirement specifically to work on the project, thus guaranteeing that the new kettles for Sierra Nevada's expanded brewhouse shared the same ancestral heritage as their predecessors.

Much of the newly acquired brewing equipment, including the kettles, had been prefabricated in Germany. This meant that the actual assembly of appliances would not need to take place on site; however, it was important that the shell of the new building be ready for the arrival of the prefabricated brewing equipment. The man responsible for the design of the new site—or West Brewhouse, as it came to be called—was Matt Gallaway, a local boy who had recently graduated from UC Berkeley with a bachelor's degree in environmental design in architecture. Whereas the original East Brewhouse had been fashioned in a Bavarian style, Gallaway and Grossman decided to lend a Mediterranean, south-of-France character to the West Brewhouse.

Its centerpiece would be a spacious brewing hall whose exterior was defined by sandstone stucco walls, a gently sloping twin-gabled roof, and two full bay windows revealing the signature copper kettles inside, along with a lauter tun and a whirlpool vessel.

Construction of the new brewhouse began in late 1997. There followed a frenetic four-month period when all the brewing equipment had to be installed. The situation was not made any easier when it was discovered that the city's main drain system—a three-and-a-half-foot-wide pipe—ran through the middle of the new site. It would need to be completely rerouted, at the company's expense, before building could begin. Nevertheless, they met their target date and the West Brewhouse opened in 1998, at the expense of $25 million. The brewery's combined production capacity was now close to 800,000 barrels per annum, capable of twelve brews a day.

By 1998, the craft beer bubble had burst. Around the nation, small breweries were closing with regularity. Many of them had failed to heed a lesson that Grossman and Camusi had emphasized from the outset: the pursuit of quality mattered more than shortcuts and quick profits. A surplus of new breweries, many of which were producing less than average beers, contributed to a glut of mediocre beers. In fact, according to *Consumer Reports* in its June 1996 edition, many of the microbrewed beers at this time were "flawed and stale-tasting." Evidently, a long overdue shakeout was in order. Yet because Sierra Nevada had stuck to its core values of quality and consistency, it would not only survive the shakeout, it would also be seen increasingly as a company that could point the way for the future of the craft-brewing industry.

THE BUYOUT OF PAUL CAMUSI

O N THE surface, exciting developments were taking place at the brewery. Housed in a brand new, state-of-the-art facility, the company was making handsome profits and was growing in popularity around the nation. But, beneath the surface, an ongoing tension was playing out which, when combined with the bursting of the craft brew bubble in the mid-'90s, presented the stiffest test for the company to date. Ken Grossman characterizes this period as "one of the most difficult, challenging, and stressful points in my life."

Since 1991, Grossman had approached Camusi for a possible buyout. Even though they were partners in the business, it was clear to everyone concerned that Grossman was putting in disproportionate amounts of time and energy. Camusi seemed to be increasingly disengaged. In fact, he was not even turning up to work on some days. Now that Sierra Nevada was no longer a semi-amateurish hobbyist's dream, it appeared that Camusi had lost his passion for the enterprise.

Camusi initially expressed an interest in an early buyout. Ironically, however, the very success that seemed to diminish his zest for running the business also made it more difficult for a quick and tidy buyout. Camusi's lawyers advised their client to hold out as long as he could while the value of the company continued to climb; in this way, he would eventually be able to cash in his chips for a larger pot of money.

The lawyers even put pressure on Grossman to follow the lead of competitors by aligning with a big brewer or going public on the stock market. This would have raised quick money which he needed—firstly to buy out Camusi, secondly to fund the $25 million expansion project.

"What are we going to do with the future of the company?" That was the question consuming Grossman. To this day, it's still a painful topic for him to discuss, as I noticed on several occasions during interviews.

He considered his options. He could allow himself to be bought out by bigger companies such as Anheuser-Busch or even a foreign-owned brewery such as Heineken whose CEO met with Grossman to discuss a deal but Grossman came away from the meeting unimpressed. In fact, his mind was already made up. "I wasn't interested in having another partner," he now freely admits. "And I didn't feel it would be the right direction for the company to be involved with a major brewer."

He could also explore venture funding but this would require owing debt capital to the loan company, something that did not sit well with Grossman's astute business ethics.

A third possibility was suggested by an attorney from San Francisco whose advice Grossman particularly trusted. Put simply, it was this: "Why don't you see if you can borrow 100 percent of it and pay it off in five years?"

He put a deal together with a local branch of Wells Fargo Bank. The year was 1997 and the craft beer bubble was bursting. Camusi's attorneys "saw the writing on the wall," as Grossman puts it. They thought it would be a good time to settle.

They agreed to a deal. "I started to panic," says Grossman, "because the marketplace was softening up and I began to hear a lot of gloom and doom stories about the craft movement and here I'd just heavily leveraged myself, assuming there would be continued growth rather than a flattening or decline. I leveraged myself to the max with several different layers of debit. This kind of thing would be impossible today."

Fortunately, Sierra Nevada avoided serious fallout from the bursting of the craft beer bubble. "But if it had gone the other way, I would have really struggled," admits Grossman. "It was a very hairy period. I had played all my cards, and I was hoping that in the end, it would turn out all right."

A buyout settlement was finally reached in early 1999.

Camusi has since cut all connections with the brewery but continues to live in Chico. When I tried to locate him, as part of my research for this book, I was surprised that no one at the brewery could give me his address—even though some knew roughly where he lived, and others had occasionally spotted him around town. I conducted an Internet search but all I could ascertain was that he races Porsches for a semipro motor sports team. I was beginning to despair of ever contacting him and hearing his side of the Sierra Nevada story. Eventually, I discovered his address because of a political contribution he made in the 2008 presidential campaign (available through the Public Records Office). I wrote him a letter asking for an interview but several weeks went by without a response. I even drove by his house in hopes of spotting him out in the front yard. However, I'm an academic not a journalist—so I didn't knock on his door, out of respect for his privacy.

Then, on a Tuesday morning in April 2010, as I'm preparing for a class at Chico State, my office telephone rings. "Hello, this is Paul Camusi," he says. The voice is assertive yet somewhat restrained, and I detect a hint of tired cynicism as he talks. "I'd prefer if we just speak on the phone rather than in person," he says, and I go along with the request. *If this means being late for my class then so be it*, I reason to myself. *I'm sure my students will understand.* As the telephone conversation continues, I sense that, for Camusi, the days of Sierra Nevada are past and gone forever; he prefers not to dwell on them. Instead, he steers the conversation to his plans for the future. "I've always been an entrepreneur," he tells me. His latest ventures include farming an 800-acre walnut orchard in Arbuckle (fifty miles south of Chico) and managing a small vineyard and homestead in Napa Valley, where he enjoys cultivating Bordeaux grapes. "I prefer wine to beer these days," he says with resignation and an undercurrent of bitterness. The idealist in me would love to suggest a reunion with Ken Grossman at the Taproom over a few beers; but I'm realistic enough to know this is as impossible as getting John Lennon and Paul McCartney back together again for one last hurrah.

On the eve of the new millennium, as Sierra Nevada Brewing Co. approached its twentieth anniversary, Ken Grossman became the sole owner and CEO of the company. He had endured the most serious challenges of his life to date. His singular vision could now express itself.

Scenes from the Taproom, Part III
April 10, 2009: Bob Littell, The Public Face of Sierra Nevada

T he Taproom is where the public goes to have a drink, a meal, enjoy good company, or relax after taking a brewery tour. For some, it's the destination point of their pilgrimage to Chico; sitting at the bar, they can enjoy a view of the two shiny copper kettles that are the heart and soul of the brewing operation. It's the place where you'll see employees on lunch break or hanging out after a work shift. If you're a local, chances are you have your own beer stein or mug tucked away in one of the glass-door cabinets behind the bar. It's also where new beers, mostly from the 10-barrel Pilot Brewery, are tasted and tested on a regular basis.

The manager of this space, since 1997, is Bob Littell. In 2000, after the opening of the Big Room as a concert venue, he effectively had control over both bookends of the Sierra Nevada brewery—the Taproom and Restaurant on the east side and the Big Room on the west side. I visit him on a spring morning. We sit in a clean, rather nondescript office space, far removed from the Taproom. As I soon discover, Bob is all business, and that means no drinking while on the job. In fact, the only drink on hand is filtered water.

"I am the public face of Sierra Nevada," he says. It's not intended as a boast. He thinks carefully about his word choices. He is slim, sharp-witted, and fit for his age, early sixties. This is not surprising seeing that he used to run several miles every day until a left knee replacement put an end to his running regimen. He enjoys the occasional tipple but he's not a big drinker and certainly not when he's on the job. He admits that when he wakes up every morning, he can't wait to get to work.

Halfway through our interview, he pauses and reflects. He's been talking a lot. I've been listening. "Excuse me for my verbal expansiveness," he apologizes. "It's just that I love to talk about this place." It's an understandable problem, I point out.

A consummate professional, a musician first and foremost, Bob Littell was formerly married to Laura Joplin, sister of legendary vocalist, Janis. Music colors his life. He grew up in the Haight-Ashbury district of San Francisco in the 1960s and went to school with Bill Kreutzmann (drummer for the Grateful Dead) and Greg Rolie (organist and lead singer for the original Santana, formed in 1967).

"Check YouTube," he says. "You're more likely to see a video of me there than Ken Grossman." So I checked and discovered that what he says is true. Not only do you find videos of Bob Littell introducing world-class musical acts for Sierra Center Stage (a series of concerts in the Big Room aired on public television), but you also see him playing harmonica on stage with luminaries such as guitar wizard, Tommy Emmanuel.

Bob Littell is a fitting symbol for the brewery: energetic, passionate about his calling, and an accomplished artisan. But the story of Sierra Nevada is inevitably much more than Bob Littell. In fact, a more appropriate symbol for Sierra Nevada Brewing Co. might be its Taproom and Restaurant: in particular, the comfortable spaciousness of the open dining room, the plush seating, the copper ducts that crisscross the vaulted ceiling, the vibrant flowers and plants tastefully displayed in corners and on shelves, and outside, a shaded patio with a Zen garden vibe. After all, this is the reason why so many customers, like me, keep coming back to the place. And on that point, Bob Littell would surely be hard pressed to disagree.

CHAPTER FOUR

In Pursuit of Hop Harmony
2000–2010

FOOTPRINTS

AFTER THE craft brewing bubble burst in the late 1990s, many smaller breweries fell by the wayside. Not so, Sierra Nevada. Because of a loyal customer base, demand was stronger than ever. However, its popularity was still limited mainly to the West Coast. In fact, at the turn of the millennium, more than half of Sierra Nevada beer was sold in California and, of that amount, 43 percent was purchased in the northern half of the state.

The story of the next decade would see a significant growth in the Sierra Nevada brand profile—across the nation, even across the oceans. This expansion took on different guises: from the cultural (with the opening of a showcase auditorium, the Big Room), to the ecological (with the adoption of an increasingly sustainable brewing agenda) and the socio-political (with due recognition of the brewery and of Ken Grossman by various agencies and institutions from the governor of California to California State University, Chico). Throughout this period, the company's repertoire of beers also expanded with the advent of bolder styles and the introduction of innovative brewing techniques.

To accommodate this all-round expansion, it was necessary to increase the physical footprint of the brewery site and Grossman opportunely acquired two neighboring properties on 20th Street: a disused nut processing plant and an abandoned amusement park previously known as Fun World. A major remodeling of the Taproom and Restaurant was undertaken in early 2000, followed by an extension of parking facilities on the east side of the brewery. The total footprint of the brewery eventually reached close to forty acres.

Ironically, this expansion profile would interact with a countervailing agenda: contraction of the company's ecological footprint. Even though it's an agenda that Sierra Nevada Brewing Co. had embraced from its inception, the challenge now was how to maintain such an agenda while still pursuing an ambitious growth rate.

The answer to the challenge gradually evolved into a core principle: "hop harmony." This phrase would become the mantra that embodied Sierra Nevada's holistic philosophy about brewing and the world: an intricately interconnected ecosystem, a closed loop, whereby resources and materials are used responsibly in honor of the final product—flavorful beer of the highest quality.

Y2K

O N NEW Year's Eve, 2000, a more immediate challenge presented itself, in the form of Y2K. Like most business owners at the time, Ken Grossman had some trepidation about the turn of the millennium scenario—how a glitch in computer chips would lead to a breakdown of automated processes, from brewing equipment to accounting services. Around the globe, there was a widespread fear that the operating number systems on computers would not recognize the last two numbers 00 in the year 2000—the so-called millennium bug—and that this would result in the shutdown of the entire power grid with lights going off all over the world, planes falling out of the sky, and nuclear weapons being accidentally triggered.

As it turned out, these apocalyptic fears were misplaced. Nevertheless, the episode illustrated the extent to which our lives had become dependent on technology by the year 2000. Breweries, in particular, were reliant on computerization and automation for a full range of functions—from the brewing process to the cleaning of equipment, from accounting to marketing, from personal communication to information sharing. Indeed, the term microbrewery was originally borrowed from the world of micro computing technology.

For Sierra Nevada, the turning point had been 1998 with the addition of the West Brewhouse, twice the size of the original plant. With size and advanced technology came increasing levels of automation—control platforms and intricate software programs that commanded every step of the brewing process.

Now that the brewery was running 24/7, it could not afford to shut down. Unlike a computer, it could not simply be rebooted in the event of a catastrophic failure. So Grossman proceeded to do what any good captain would do to protect his ship from disaster. He developed and enacted a proactive plan. He installed a standby generator so that, if the grid was disabled by Y2K, he could temporarily run the brewery off its own power. He bought a 35,000-gallon propane tank and created a system that could run off propane gas instead of the natural gas normally distributed by PG&E. And he worked out a contingency plan with California Water Service in the event that his water supply might be shut off.

On New Year's Eve, 1999, Grossman was not partying around Chico. He was at the brewery, taking command, and waiting nervously for the countdown to midnight, ready to step in and launch his emergency preparedness plan if necessary. Fourteen-year-old Brian accompanied his father, breathing in the adventure as only an impressionable teenager knows how, and blissfully unaware of the anxiety felt by his father and the skeleton crew on hand that night.

Ironically, as all of us living in California were soon to find out, surviving the Y2K scare was the least of our energy concerns. Rolling power blackouts and power shortages became the norm throughout 2000 while energy bills skyrocketed. Simply put: the state was suffering from a shortage of electricity (exacerbated by price-gouging activities on the energy market). Even though California's energy crisis was eventually resolved in late 2003 when a state of emergency was lifted, Grossman learned an important lesson from the meltdown: his company needed to attain greater energy self-sufficiency. A more aggressive strategy was required if Sierra Nevada was ever to delink entirely from an unstable and unreliable power grid. Grossman was to spend the rest of the decade meeting this challenge with typical ingenuity and astute long-term planning.

THE BIG ROOM

FEARS OF near-catastrophe around the world quickly turned to grounds for celebration at the brewery when, a few months later, a 350-seat auditorium, the Big Room, was opened on the west side of the facility. Designed as a social space for meetings, fundraising events, and concerts, the capacious auditorium lent a distinctive and dignified ambiance to the west side of the brewhouse, a mirror of sorts to the east side flanked by the ever-popular Taproom and Restaurant. The Big Room was quick to win over admirers. "Acoustically brilliant and dripping with elegance," wrote one reviewer, "the room is an immaculate environment for the exchange between player and listener." Over the years, the Big Room has continued to earn praise not just because of the quality of music performed there but also because of the auditorium's majestic appearance, distinguished by its soft ambient lighting, dark wood paneling, and gracefully curved room dividers.

The opening of the Big Room in 2000 held a special significance for Grossman. He had grown up loving music. His dad played guitar. As a teenager, he had enjoyed attending rock concerts at Valley Music Theatre on Ventura Boulevard, just down the road from his home in Woodland Hills. Jimi Hendrix, Buffalo Springfield, and Fleetwood Mac were amongst those he had the chance to go and watch before the theatre closed down (it subsequently reopened as a Jehovah's Witness assembly-hall). The opportunity to share his passion for eclectic styles of music appealed to Grossman. Since 1989, the Taproom and Restaurant had hosted Monday night concerts ("pub parties," as they came to be known) on a small makeshift stage, featuring bands mainly from the West Coast. Even though the concerts were always popular (and continued until their eventual demise in 2010), a larger auditorium was always the pipe dream. Grossman thought of calling it "The Jazz Club" and wanted it modeled on the popular Bay Area venue, Yoshi's. He envisioned a comfortable space where concertgoers could enjoy fine dining and quality beer while being treated to music facilitated by a state-of-the-art sound system.

Ricky Skaggs and Kentucky Thunder at the Big Room

In late 2002, Grossman handed the Big Room over to Bob Littell and said, "Bob, you work out the specifics." In 2004, it would receive national exposure on public television with the program *Sierra Center Stage*—a thirteen-part public television series (modeled on the popular *Austin City Limits),* featuring well-known artists from the world of folk, blues, and jazz such as Richard Thompson, Tommy Emmanuel, Bela Fleck, Roy Rogers, Nickel Creek, and Sonia Dada. To this date, the Big Room continues to attract a mix of musical artists who are at the peak of their musical careers or just starting out. Chances are, you might not have heard of Baskery (an all-female Swedish bluegrass band) or The Fabulous Swing Kings (a local dance ensemble specializing in tunes from the Big Band era), but after an evening's performance at the Big Room, their reputations typically receive the equivalent of a Colbert bump.

QUALITY AND INNOVATION

CONSISTENT WITH its past history, Sierra Nevada continued to expand in the fields of research and development, brewing technology, and innovation. Grossman had never forgotten his early problems with aeration and oxidation that resulted in having to throw out his first ten batches of beer. He was particularly sensitive to the need for beer consistency and the problem of oxygen pick-up during the bottling process. Since 1997, there had been a small quality control lab at the brewery whose role was to detect and correct deficiencies. But a more aggressive strategy was needed if the company was going to keep up to date with cutting-edge research and emerging technologies. In 2004, a 500-square-foot research and development lab was built alongside a 10-barrel Pilot Brewery. Their collective charge: to conduct a qualitative-based analysis on all aspects of the brewing process. This would be both practical and theoretical in nature.

Gil Sanchez was hired in May 2004 as the head of R&D. A

chemical engineer by training, Sanchez came to Sierra Nevada from Miller Brewing Company where he had been asked to research, amongst other things, special techniques for producing "clear beer" and storing beer in plastic bottles. Now at Sierra Nevada, he has the opportunity, he informs me, to work on what he calls "real" beer projects: the Torpedo process (a pioneering method of harnessing hop oils and resins), special techniques for stabilizing aroma quality, and ways of analyzing the fruity esters in Kellerweis (a wheat beer that began year-round production in 2009). He confesses to getting a thrill from using state-of-the-art analytical instruments "in order to understand beer." To a layman like me, this at first seems slightly absurd, even perverse. What is there to understand about beer? But after spending thirty minutes talking with Gil Sanchez, you begin to appreciate how efficiently his brilliantly analytical mind breaks beer down into minute categories (such as basic chemical structures and molecular formulae). His job is to probe these mysteries.

Gil tells me that his department has two distinctive yet overlapping roles: reactive and proactive. The reactive function involves problem solving and answering questions and concerns, from packaging to shipping to fermenting and finishing. Defect testing takes place twice a month when members of the brewery evaluate samples of beer (at 11:00 in the morning) in order to identify compounds that may or may not enhance the flavor profile of given beers. For example, if the levels of diacetyl are too high, then the beer can taste like butter, or if there is too much butyric acid then the beer will taste like baby sick or sour milk. Dotted around the lab are state-of-the-art machines, including a gas chromatography mass spectrometer and olfactometer with a combined value of around $250,000. These are used for analyzing beer aroma qualities, allowing lab assistants to monitor aroma profile in a matrix: from catty to leathery, sweet to sour, malty to hoppy, skunky to smoky. There's also a high performance liquid chromatographer for analyzing degrees of bitterness produced by compounds such as hop alpha acids and also to help regulate the amount of wort sugars required by yeast for optimum fermentation. These machines notwithstanding, human testing and tasting are still the main methods for discovering flaws. This is the sensory-based approach to brewing: allowing the brewer to identify and isolate desirable flavors and smells, then use more of them as required.

The other side of R&D is proactive: to engage in new product development, and to experiment with new ideas. For example, Steve Dresler, brewmaster at the main brewery, might come up with a concept, and then go to Scott Jennings, head brewer at the Pilot Brewery, to try it out. As the 10-barrel Pilot Brewery is a miniature replica of the West Brewhouse (one-twentieth of its size), it's perfectly suited for experiments that can be scaled up to the main brewery. Two innovative styles, in particular, have resulted from this creative synergy: a Bavarian style wheat beer (Kellerweis) and an Extra India Pale Ale (Torpedo). Says Dresler: "There's nothing nicer than going over to your pub, the local next door, and saying, 'This is my beer.' It doesn't get much better than

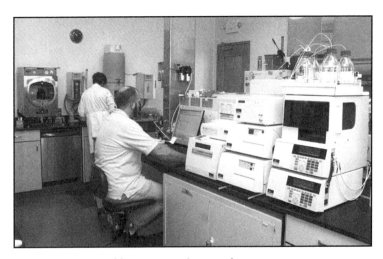

Research and development lab assistant Aaron Porter uses the spectrometer

that, and I've so enjoyed that."

Scott Jennings graduated with a brewmaster's diploma from the Versuchs-und Lehranstalt fur Brauerei in Berlin (VLB), a brewing program affiliated with the Berlin University of Technology. He smiles a lot: maybe it's because he loves his job so much, for which I can't blame him. At a time when automated technology predominates in any modern brewery, he gets to do more hands-on brewing in his Pilot Brewery than probably anyone else at Sierra Nevada. In the middle of showing me around his gleaming facility, he halts abruptly by a bright beer tank, then right out of the blue, he tells me that he's always been fascinated by Joseph Conrad's novel, *Heart of Darkness*.

I'm taken aback. It's one of the hardest novels I was ever assigned at graduate school—a torturous story about a tortured soul, famously adapted into the blockbuster film *Apocalypse Now* by Francis Ford Coppola who changed the historical setting of the novel from colonial Africa to war-torn Vietnam.

"Why the fascination?" I ask.

His smile transforms into a look of stern seriousness. "Because

Scott Jennings and the Pilot Brewery

Conrad agonized over every word," he says. It occurs to me that for all the science involved in making beer, brewers like Scott Jennings are preoccupied by a key fundamental question: how to create a work of art that will endure forever.

W HEN ROB Fraser, a modest Canadian with a lean, athletic build, was hired in May 2007 to supervise quality control issues, he was quickly introduced to another major preoccupation at the brewery—the danger of oxygen ingress in bottles. Grossman wanted to switch from twist-off caps to pry-off caps with a liner in the cap that helped to seal the bottle. He had asked R&D specialists to examine the issue: after one year of extensive research, they concluded that pry-off caps were better for the beer and for shelf life because they prevented oxygen from seeping into the bottle. Oxygen ingress occurred six times more with twist-offs than pry-offs, they reported. Therefore, in late 2007, Grossman made the decision to restructure his entire bottling line to accommodate pry-off caps. This proved costly, both in terms of time and money. It was also deeply unpopular amongst those beer drinkers who liked the convenience of using their wrists rather than a bottle opener to pour their beer.

According to Grossman, Sierra Nevada received more angry e-mails on the pry-off topic than any other in the history of the company. To the newly-hired Fraser, the episode was an eye-opener. He had previously worked for the multinational conglomerate InBev in Ontario. He now realized that his new boss observed a very different mantra from his previous employers: "Quality over cost." For the industrial brewers, notes Fraser, high volume is always the bottom line. For smaller companies like Sierra Nevada Brewing Co., it's all about respect, integrity, and doing the right thing, he says. "[Grossman] cares about the consumer as much as his own people," he goes on to say.

There's a curious twist to this topic which Rob Fraser presents to me in the form of a riddle: "Ken Grossman is prepared to take hits to profit margins in order to improve quality but ends up making money." In other words, "virtue will be rewarded." It's a moral lesson that appeals to me, right up there with "Do the right thing and good things happen." As it turns out, moving from twist-off caps to pry-offs was simply the right thing to do and even though it proved unpopular with some consumers at first, the improvement in beer quality and shelf life as result of the change won more admirers in the long term.

Another good example of doing the right thing is the agenda of sustainable brewing, a predominant leitmotif at the brewery since its early beginnings.

SUSTAINABLE BREWING

IN 2005, Sierra Nevada Brewing Co. was recognized by the state of California for its environmental stewardship earning the Governor's Environmental and Economic Leadership Award for Sustainable Practices. As part of his administration's promotion of renewable energy sources, Governor Arnold Schwarzenegger wanted to recognize and applaud Ken Grossman's attempts to move away from a carbon-based energy platform, in particular Sierra Nevada's recent acquisition of hydrogen fuel cells, capable of meeting more than half of the company's energy needs. The governor's visit to Chico brought with it the usual high security—snipers on the rooftops of the brewery and bodyguards placed strategically around the plant. At the end of the tour and award ceremony, neckties were loosened and drinks poured. Schwarzenegger enjoyed his pint of lager. "He's a genuine beer drinker," says Grossman of the governor.

Why did Grossman win the leadership award for sustainable practices? Perhaps it's best to begin with his personal philosophy and perspective on the world. "Sustainability," he tells me, "has been our lifestyle—my wife's and mine—for over thirty-five years. We've had a compost heap, raised our chickens, and had gardens. We have been connected with that culture even before we built the brewery (on Gilman Way). Then as I built the brewery, I was forced to be resourceful because I couldn't do anything else. So I spent a lot of days rummaging through scrap yards to build the first brewery. That was my mind-set from day one: to figure out how to do things simply, and then that agenda grew as I began to understand how things worked."

In other words, "reduce, reuse, and recycle" was always the operating mantra at Sierra Nevada. To this day, its sustainability program touches every facet of the brewery's operation, from heating to cooling, from brewing to packaging, from cultivation of raw materials to disposal of waste. It diverts as much as 99.5 percent of solid waste from landfills. It regularly receives honorary mentions from California's Waste Reduction Award Program

Walking the talk: Governor Schwarzenegger and Ken Grossman discuss renewable energy at the 2005 Sustainability Award held at the brewery

(WRAP). It reuses spent brewing materials such as yeast, hops, and grain as a nutritional supplement for a herd of approximately sixty cows at the nearby University Farm which provides 600–800 pounds of beef a week for the Restaurant. It even trades with local beekeepers: they receive hop burlap sacks in return for providing the Restaurant with honey.

The brewing process generates huge amounts of heat; in addition, fermentation produces high volumes of carbon dioxide, a greenhouse gas. As far back as the 1990s, heat recovery systems had been installed throughout the brewery to capture and recycle heat whenever possible, rather than allowing it to leak into the atmosphere. In 1997 vapor condensers were installed on the brew kettles to increase efficiency and recover steam from the boiling process. Later, in 2005, a carbon dioxide recovery system was installed that diverted the carbon dioxide gas (produced during natural fermentation) to the packaging plant where it can be used for carbonation in the bottling process and for keg pressurization. A series of technology upgrades has continued to increase energy efficiency and minimize air emissions.

The brewery is one of Chico's biggest users of water. Until 2002, it relied on the city for wastewater management. Then it installed its own wastewater treatment facility, an anaerobic and aerobic digester, that removes 95 percent of unwanted materials (such as organics and contaminants) before the water is discharged safely or is used to irrigate the on-site hop field during the hot summer months. Later, it added a biogas compressor that would feed methane-rich biogas into the boiler system.

Sierra Nevada's energy workhorse is the stack of fuel cells, so admired by Governor Schwarzenegger during his visit to Chico. These cells, commissioned in 2005, make up one of the largest cogeneration fuel cell power plants in the United States. A fuel cell is an electrochemical device, similar to a battery, which uses hydrogen and oxygen to produce electricity. Unlike a battery, however, the fuel cell never dies, nor does it produce toxic pollutants as a byproduct. Instead, the chemical reactions inside the cell generate (in addition to an electric current) hot air and water, both of which can be captured and used for other applications (such as heating the brew kettles). In other words, fuel cell technology is efficient and clean. It's not cheap, however, which is why the technology is still in its infancy and has yet to attain full commercial application. With help from a $2.4 million PG&E rebate and $1 million funding from the U.S. Department of Defense, Grossman was able to finance the purchase of four 250-kilowatt fuel cell power units producing one megawatt of power (enough to power 1,000 homes for a year). He also calculated that the money he personally invested in the cells would be recouped within a seven-year time frame.

In December 2006, Sierra Nevada voluntarily joined the California Climate Action Registry, reporting its greenhouse gas emissions and recording daily statistics on its website (*www.sierranevada.com*). The website also tracks the amount of energy being

The hydrogen fuel cells: Sierra Nevada's energy workhorse, producing enough electricity to power 1,000 homes for a year

The solar array covering rooftops and parking lot

generated at the brewery, and whether or not the plant is feeding electricity back to the power grid for that particular day.

In 2008, a biodiesel processor was acquired, allowing the company to convert the restaurant's spent cooking oil into biodiesel fuel for use in the local and long-haul fleet of delivery trucks.

That same year, construction of one of the nation's largest privately-owned solar arrays was completed. Three acres of these panels are capable of tracking the sun as it arcs across the sky and are placed over Sierra Nevada's public parking lot (thereby also providing shade for customer vehicles); the remainder of the photovoltaic panels (10,000 in all) adorn the majority of the brewing facility's rooftops. In total, these solar panels generate 1.5 MW ac of clean, emissions-free power.

As part of its mission to make a "locavore beer" out of locally sourced materials, a three-acre hop field had been planted in 2003, reviving a proud hop-growing tradition in the Sacramento

The hop field

Valley before other cash crops took over. Since 2003, the field has expanded to nine acres and the quality of hops has improved with each harvest. Hops are particularly thirsty plants; consequently, Sierra Nevada has needed to adopt an innovative strategy for re-use of its own water on the field. About a mile from the brewery, twenty-six acres of barley were planted in 2008 and harvested in spring 2009 for the first Harvest Estate Ale.

Next to this barley field, a rail spur was completed in 2009, together with one mile of specially-built railroad track and an unloading station, allowing grains shipped from Canada to be transported by train on Southern Pacific Railroad rather than semi-trailers. Three or four truckloads of grain are shipped in one rail car. Once the goods have been delivered by train to Chico, they are then transferred from railroad car to truck for the final leg to the brewery. This is far more eco-friendly, reducing the carbon footprint by approximately 30 percent.

CHERI CHASTAIN was hired in September 2006 as sustainability coordinator. She has a master's degree from Chico State in environmental geography. Her task is to bring cohesiveness to the sustainability agenda and to ensure that it is applied comprehensively during Sierra Nevada's ongoing expansion. It's a position she takes seriously, judging from the big blue exercise ball she uses as an office chair and the extensive "To Do" list next to her desk. Here are the issues she's working on when I interview her in spring 2009: (1) the Green Machine (providing incentives for employees to bike to work); (2) the compost heap (converting solid waste materials such as filter pads, coffee grounds, food scraps, and spent grain into more than a ton of rich, organic matter); (3) the biodiesel project (converting waste vegetable oil from the restaurant into fuel for the transportation fleet); (4) a greenhouse gas inventory (in cooperation with the California Climate Registry); (5) the worm bin (using earthworms to make fertilizer and compost).

Cheri Chastain is enthusiastic about her calling. She believes passionately in the noble ideal of 100 percent self-generated energy. As the recycling "czar" she also makes sure that everything—

The unloading station

from burlap sacks to batteries and bubble-wrap—are placed in their proper recycling bins.

Her favorite mantra is "closing the loop." She breaks this down for me by explaining its three parts: first, what's coming into the plant (the raw materials); second, processing (the use of heat, water, steam, and electricity to make the beer); third, waste disposal (reusing and recycling as much as possible and only resorting to throwing away when absolutely necessary). In this way, both upstream and downstream are looked after, she tells me with a satisfied smile.

In recognition of its long-standing adherence to a green ethic, Sierra Nevada won the Sustainable Plant of the Year Award from *Food Engineering* magazine in 2009.

A TRAGIC EPISODE

IN AUGUST 2007, tragedy struck with the death of Steve Harrison, at the age of 54. Harrison was the first employee to be hired by Grossman and Camusi in 1981. Over the years he rose to become vice president of Sierra Nevada Brewing Co., responsible for marketing and distribution as well as production planning. His high profile guaranteed that the story of his death stayed on the front pages of the local newspaper for several weeks. On many levels, it's a story that is still shrouded in mystery.

What we do know is this: Harrison had been dealing with stress issues partly because of transitions at the company involving reorganization of management structure, and partly because of recurring physical ailments, particularly weak knees for which he was taking prescription painkillers. This was tough for someone who loved to exercise in the outdoors, especially going on long bike rides with friends from Chico Velo, the local bike club.

On Tuesday, August 7, he failed to show up at work. Later that day, his blue Toyota Prius was found abandoned parked alongside the Sacramento River, about five miles outside Chico.

It was unlocked. There was no sign of a body anywhere close by, but a discarded prescription bottle was later found a along the river's edge. Ken Grossman and close family members were alerted. Grossman retrieved the Prius and drove it to the police station where it was examined for evidence. A sheriff's helicopter was used that afternoon to patrol the river area. Grossman spread the word quickly and gave permission for workers to go on an extensive search mission along the river. The brewery was reduced to a skeleton staff on that day—one of the only occasions in twenty-seven years when this happened (other than on a public holiday). Patrol boats and park rangers joined the search effort along with rescue dogs. At this point, nothing was ruled out: foul play, accident, suicide. An intensive search followed. Finally, on Friday, August 17, ten days since he had gone missing, a local resident, out on a Jet Ski, found Harrison's body under a snag, about half a mile from where his car had been abandoned.

The local newspaper carried his obituary: "Steve enjoyed a lifelong sense of curiosity and loved literature, fine films, and spirited conversation. He was devoted to the Chico community and appreciated its beauty, opportunities, and citizenry." The Steve Harrison Memorial Bikeway was dedicated to him several months later, opened by the mayor of Chico; fittingly, it was a bike route leading from town to fabled Honey Run Road. A fund was established in his name to promote environmental sustainability and alternative energy projects.

(Later that same year, Ed McLaughlin, who had worked briefly at the brewery in its nascent stages, was involved in a bike crash that caused a catastrophic spinal-cord injury leaving him severely paralyzed. His bike collided with a metal bollard, a divider in the middle of the road in Lower Bidwell Park. Once again, the biking and beer community rallied to his cause—organizing a fundraiser, "Tour de Ed," through the park, to help with his extensive hospital and rehabilitation expenses).

BOLD NEW DIRECTIONS

I T WAS impossible to fill Steve Harrison's shoes. As one beer
blogger wrote: "Steve carried perhaps the greatest institu-
tional knowledge of craft beer distribution and understanding of the complex state-by-state political and legislative land-
scape than anyone else in the industry." Nevertheless, even before
his death, a shift towards greater emphasis on brand management
and customer feedback was already taking place at the brewery.
The previous year, the position of director of sales and marketing
was taken by Joe Whitney, who had spent eighteen years in sales
and brand stewardship at Boston Beer Company and New Belgium Brewing Company. Bill Manley was brought in as communications coordinator principally to oversee discussions and beer
reviews related to Sierra Nevada on blogs, websites, and other
web-based communications. Theresa Hildebrand, who had previously worked in quality control, was transitioned to answer consumer concerns and complaints.

By the end of 2007, two of Ken Grossman's three children
were also ready to take a more active role in the business: Sierra
as brand manager (emphasizing brand profile and market niche)
and Brian as supervisor of brewery operations (a position with
a range of responsibilities including supervision of local distribution). Sierra had started out as a dishwasher at the brewery's
restaurant, Brian as a cleaner of fermentation tanks; both had dil-
igently worked their way up to management positions. More recently, the youngest daughter, Carrie, assumed a role in communications at the brewery. As members of CBG2 (Craft Brewing
Generation 2)—children of parents who helped launch the craft-
brewing revolution—they represent the future not only of Sierra Nevada Brewing Co. but also, along with peers such as Brett
Joyce of Rogue Brewing (located in Newport, Oregon) and Laura
Bell of Bell's Brewing Co. (located in Kalamazoo, Michigan), the
future of the craft-brewing industry as a whole.

A greater emphasis was clearly being placed on expanding the brand profile of Sierra Nevada—in other words, how the company was perceived by its core customers. In particular, its reputation for making pale ale and predominantly hoppy beers—while solid and secure in its own way—was deemed somewhat limiting and restrictive. A wider repertoire of beers was desired. For the first time in its history, Sierra Nevada embarked on a quick succession of new, experimental beer styles to go along with its proven favorites.

Commenting on the creative resurgence that followed, brewmaster Steve Dresler tells me in spring 2009: "It's been pretty hot and heavy recently, after a lull." He then goes on to list some of the breakthrough styles that have been recently released: ESB (an English bitter), Torpedo Extra IPA (a special India pale ale), the Harvest Series (featuring freshly-harvested hops from different growing regions of the world), Kellerweis (a hefeweizen wheat beer), and Glissade (a golden bock lager). The stories of Harvest, Torpedo, and Kellerweis, in particular, are worth telling.

Harvest Series. Since 1996, Grossman had wanted to make a series of beers that followed the hop harvest around the world. The challenge was to bring freshly-picked "wet" hops to the brewery so they could be added immediately to the brew kettles while still fresh and lively. Three hop-growing regions were eventually chosen: the Yakima Valley in eastern Washington (whose Cascade and Centennial hops have traditionally been a staple of Sierra Nevada beers), a southern hemisphere location in the Nelson region of New Zealand's South Island (producers of Pacific Hallertau, Motueka, and Southern Cross hops), and Chico (using hops from Sierra Nevada's own hop field).

The result was the Harvest series of three hop-heavy beers: a cornerstone Harvest Ale (released every April), a Southern Hemisphere Harvest (released every October), and more recently an Estate Brewers Harvest Ale (released in late fall, featuring locally-grown hops and barley that capture local flavors and earth tones, or "terroir" as winemakers like to call it).

Torpedo Extra IPA. Sierra Nevada has always believed in using whole-cone hops rather than hop extracts or pellets. The style of beer that optimally expresses hop character and robustness is India pale ale (IPA), a bolder and more assertive version of Pale Ale. Surprisingly, the brewery had never featured an IPA beer as part of its year-round repertoire. That all changed in 2009 with the launch of Torpedo Extra IPA: the name derives not from its ballistic strength (although at 7.2 percent alcohol by volume, it packs a considerable punch), but rather from the medium-sized stainless steel vessels—shaped like torpedoes—that are used to dry-hop the beer. The idea, conceived by Grossman and then tested at the Pilot Brewery before being scaled up to the main brewery, was to pack the torpedo cylinders with whole-cone hops, then circulate wort through the hops for two to three days. There

The Torpedo vessels

are two distinct advantages to this process of dry-hopping: first, it is less demanding of fermentation tanks (normal dry-hopping requires approximately eighteen days of tank use); second, it harnesses the hop oils and resins more efficiently and fully, adding to the complexity of citrus, pine, and herbal flavors and lending a more powerful aroma to the beer.

Kellerweis. One style of beer particularly favored by Grossman is Hefeweizen: a wheat beer that is low in hops but defined instead by refreshing, fruity flavors rendered by a wild yeast. In order to understand the beer more fully, Grossman, along with a team of brewers from Sierra Nevada (Steve Dresler, Scott Jennings, and Bart Whipple) undertook a tour of Bavarian breweries in 2008. In the town of Titting, about fifty miles north of Munich, they discovered a brewery, Guttmann Brauerei, whose head brewers, Richard Hofmeier and Gerhard Meyer, were happy to share their advice for brewing authentic Hefeweizen. This involved two principal directives: first, use the proper yeast (a specialized wild strain); second, use open fermentation tanks (allowing the yeast to build layers of flavor and aroma, not possible to do in closed tanks). The subsequent beer, named Kellerweis, was released in March 2009. One month later, as part of Chico Fest celebrations held at the brewery, Ken Grossman took the stage and launched his new beer. His intentions seemed clear: Sierra Nevada was launching more than just a new beer; it was also in the midst of launching a new portfolio of beers, expanding beyond its predominantly hop-centric profile.

JUDGING BY the range of new beers and beer styles produced at the brewery since 2009, the intention quickly translated into concrete reality. Among the list of recent beer styles are: Kolsch, Brown Saison, Golden Bock, and—in collaboration with a nearby Trappist monastery—a series of Belgian style beers due to be released in 2011.

(In addition to expanding its repertoire of beers, Sierra Nevada also experimented with mustards. Since 1998, Grossman had been interested in making a variety of condiments and sauces at the brewery for serving at the restaurant and for retail. Initially, he considered malt vinegar, grilling sauces, marinades, and mustards. When Frank Gimbel, owner of Frank's Famous Foods in the Bay Area, approached Grossman with the idea of collaborating on a series of mustards, Grossman went along with the idea. By this time, he had decided not to get distracted by food production. To this day, Sierra Nevada and Franks Famous Foods put out a range of beer-based mustards: Spicy Brown Mustard made with Porter, Stone Ground Mustard made with Stout, and Honey Spice Mustard made with Pale Ale).

As Sierra Nevada continues to expand its beer production capacity and repertoire of beer styles, it purposefully tries to stay on the cutting edge and avoid the trap of becoming over-regimented. An innovative program called Beer Camp was inaugurated in summer 2008 to help foster a culture of innovation and whimsical imagination at the brewery as well as amongst those beer aficionados around the nation wishing to attend a camp session. Roughly once every three weeks, twenty or so invited guests from different sectors of the beer industry (for example, distributors, retailers, bar owners, even homebrew enthusiasts) are treated to a two-day Willy Wonka experience around the brewery, culminating in the creation (and naming) of their own batch of beer in the 10-barrel Pilot Brewery.

As the name implies, "Beer Camp" is intended to give participants an opportunity for a beer education as well as a hands-on brewing experience; perhaps, most importantly, it also provides an excuse to indulge in unrestrained, creative thinking. An integral part of this process involves taking a tour around the brewery plant on a unique bar-bike—a cross between an oversized rickshaw and a dune buggy. Fitted with a BMW chassis, not to men-

Beer campers and the bar bike

tion a row of temperature-controlled kegs, the bike is powered by its twelve passengers who sit, pedal, and drink while being guided around the site's star attractions by Steve Grossman, Ken's oldest brother and brewery ambassador, or Terence Sullivan, assistant brewmaster and field instructor. Rather than receive a diploma or certificate at the end of the program, campers are given the ultimate reward a few weeks later, after their batch has been fermented and suitably conditioned: the beer is shipped out in kegs to all of the participants so they can enjoy the fruit of their labors with friends, family members, even customers while sharing the wondrous tale behind the beer's making.

DOCTOR GROSSMAN, WE PRESUME

O N SATURDAY, May 25, 2008, Ken Grossman was awarded an honorary doctorate of humane letters from Chico State during its annual commencement ceremony. Accepting his award from university President Paul Zingg, Grossman said with typical modesty and tight-lipped humor: "I'm especially pleased that my mother is here to attend. For most of the last thirty years, she's been asking me when I'm going to finish my degree." This was undoubtedly intended as a cheeky joke, but I can vouch for the fact that Eleanor Guy, Ken's mother, swelled with pride as she watched "young Kenny"—the tear-away teenager who built a go-kart track in his parents' backyard and a mini-brewery in his bedroom—receive his honorary hood. Several months later, when I spoke to her by phone to discuss Ken's childhood days, she still couldn't stop talking about the fact that her son was now a PhD. It was particularly poignant for her as he had never finished his degree at Butte College or Chico State. Nor had he attended his high school graduation, preferring to go backpacking in the Sierra Nevada instead.

The fact is, Ken Grossman is not the bookish type. That does not mean to say he lacks curiosity or knowledge about the world. It's as if his brain is wired not so much for written language or text but for another type of cognitive coding, particularly practical science and mechanics. As I have been told repeatedly, his genius lies in his ability to solve complex hands-on problems rather than theoretical problems.

It didn't take long for "Dr. Grossman" to produce the equivalent of his PhD thesis. As 2008 chair of the Brewers Association Technical Committee, he spearheaded a study and subsequent handbook that is widely used in all sectors of the brewing community to this day. The handbook, entitled *Draught Beer Quality Manual* offers comprehensive advice on the proper handling of beer, particularly the use of draught systems for delivering beer from brewers to consumers. Amongst the topics covered are the proper storage temperatures for kegs, an overview of the six main coupler types used to draw beer, the pros and cons of different faucet designs for pouring, the ideal levels of carbonation required to push beer, and the proper technique for pouring draught beer so as to obtain a desired one-inch collar of foam in glass. In fairness, the manual is the result of an extensive collaboration across all sectors of the brewing industry. Yet it bears Grossman's trademark signature in two distinctive ways: close attention to technical detail and critical emphasis on quality.

Charles Kyle collaborated on the writing of the *Draught Beer Quality Manual*. Kyle, a 20-year employee, started working in the restaurant at the brewery and proceeded to climb his way up. He is now in charge of security and telecommunications. I had the opportunity to attend a Power Point presentation on *Draught Beer Quality* by Charles Kyle at a brewers' conference: I never realized that a talk about jockey boxes, beer pumps, and line cleaning methods could be so enlightening and entertaining.

HOP HARMONY AT WORK: CHICO FEST, 2009

CHICO FEST, Sunday, April 26, 2009. The Sierra Nevada hop field is crawling with activity. It's a brilliant sunny spring afternoon kissed with blue skies, a light wind, and coolish temperatures in the 70s. Chico Velo's annual Wildflower one hundred-mile bike ride has just finished—a long-standing tradition attracting thousands of bikers from around the nation who relish the opportunity to pedal all day through surrounding fields and foothills. Many of them have come to the brewery after their ride, in particular to celebrate Chico Fest. The festival is part of a protracted Earth Day celebration, observed every year in Chico and normally held on the Chico State campus a couple of miles away. But today—thanks to an idea proposed by Ken Grossman's daughter, Sierra—the day has been transformed into

Chico Fest, (2009) in the hop field

a celebration of town and gown, dubbed "Chico Fest" and it's hap-
pening right here at the Sierra Nevada brewery. Local farmers
are selling a range of produce from organic vegetables to earthworms. Green business operators are touting renewable energy
sources such as solar and wind. Student organizations from the
university and community college are promoting their agendas
with eye-catching exhibition booths. Sun worshippers are gyrating to hypnotic rhythms emanating from a makeshift stage set up
on the edge of the hop field.

Moments earlier, a city of Chico forum on sustainability, held
in the Big Room and hosted by Mayor Ann Schwab, concluded
an open-door session in which members of the public discussed
all things green, from composting to clean power. Attention is
now fixed on the open-air stage. The band has stopped playing.
The joy-seekers have stopped dancing. It is time to dedicate the
recently completed solar array, now cranking out 1.5 megawatts
of power. On stage, Ken Grossman joins the mayor of Chico and
President Paul Zingg of Chico State. "The completion of the new
solar array helps bring us one step closer to our goal of one hun-

dred percent sustainable energy production," Grossman declares. He holds a glass of Kellerweis, Sierra Nevada's latest year-round release, and salutes the crowd. This is more than just a dedication, after all. It's a celebration: a toast to the values of a vibrant community, to a day well lived, and to the attainment of hop harmony.

COMING FULL CIRCLE: A CELEBRATION OF CRAFT BREW PIONEERS

A T THE end of its first thirty-year cycle, Sierra Nevada continued to expand its beer repertoire while remaining loyal to its traditional favorites. In November 2009, it released Life and Limb—a collaboration with Sam Calagione of Dogfish Head Craft Brewery (Milton, Delaware) known for his willingness to experiment with "extreme" beers. Fittingly, Life and Limb was a powerful beer, 10 percent in alcohol content, involving not only the coming together of two beer minds but also of their homegrown produce: maple syrup from Calagione's family farm in Massachusetts and hops and barley grown in the Sierra Nevada fields in Chico. It enjoyed a limited release in attractive, 24-ounce bottles, while a milder version, Limb and Life, was made available in draft only.

Calagione and Grossman wanted to collaborate on the beer as a way of honoring their ongoing friendship: both share a similar passion for craftsmanship and both pursue innovative approaches to the production of quality beers. While Grossman's rise to brewing prominence has been gradual over three decades, Calagione has earned relatively swift success with an audacious brand identity, "off-centered beer for off-centered people." The mutual respect between the two is strong in spite of their being a generation apart. Says Calagione, "It is inspiring to see a person like Ken drive a beer-centric (as opposed to a biz-centric) brewery so far and so wide while sticking to his original ideals and integrating his family into the company." Grossman reciprocates: "People like

Sam and Dogfish help to push the boundaries of beer, and it has been fun working with him and the Dogfish crew."

In early 2010, the decision was made to take the idea of collaboration beers one step further in honor of Sierra Nevada's upcoming thirtieth anniversary. A series of four specialized beers would be brewed, each with a noted pioneer of the American craft-brewing movement: Fritz Maytag of Anchor Brewing Company, Jack McAuliffe of New Albion Brewing Company, Charlie Papazian of the American Homebrewers Association, and beer guru Fred Eckhardt whose book *A Treatise on Lager Beers,* published in 1969, inspired a generation of homebrewers. As one observer put it, these were the "men who launched a thousand breweries." True to the spirit of collegiality and giving back, the collaborators agreed to donate a portion of profits from the beer to local and national charities and nonprofit organizations ranging from Chico's library system to a non-government organization (NGO) that supports indigenous peoples.

Each beer in the Sierra 30 series represented a particular chapter in the thirty-year history of Sierra Nevada Brewing Co., indeed of the American craft brewing industry as a whole. The inaugural collaboration—between Fritz Maytag and Grossman—paid tribute to the first ever batch of beer, a stout, brewed by Sierra Nevada's cofounders, Camusi and Grossman. The stout, released in March 2010, struck a fine balance between dark malty textures and lively hoppy accents; yet with an alcohol content of 9.2 percent, it was far stronger than anything deemed marketable three decades earlier. Two months later, Charlie Papazian, Fred Eckhardt, and Grossman released an Imperial Helles Bock—a lager that embodied the eclectic and experimental nature of American craft brewing. It featured a blend of Czech, Belgian, and Canadian malts; a mix of American, German, and New Zealand hops; and a combination of Sierra Nevada's home lager yeast and special yeast concocted by Papazian. Another distinguishing feature about the beer was its blend of sweetness and floral hoppiness, the result of using Sierra Nevada's unique "torpedo" method of dry-hopping. In midsummer, Jack McAuliffe and Grossman released a barley-wine harking back to the robust, flavorful ales that McAuliffe's New Albion Brewing Company once famously served as part of

The craft beer pioneers Charlie Papazian, Fritz Maytag, Ken Grossman, and Fred Eckhardt. Anchor Brewing Co., 2010. Not pictured, Jack McAuliffe

their summer solstice festivities in the late 1970s. The final release, in October, was not a collaboration but rather a marriage of Sierra Nevada's three most acclaimed beers: Bigfoot, Celebration Ale, and Pale Ale. It was called Oak Aged Ale or Our Brewer's Reserve and was guaranteed to mature with age. All the beers appeared in attractive 750 mL caged and corked bottles and had limited release, thus further adding to their mystique.

When the pioneers met in early 2010 to discuss their brewing agenda, they sat around a table at Maytag's Anchor Brewing facility in San Francisco, clinking glasses and sharing memories of the past as well as insights into the future. Eckhardt marveled at the imaginative beer styles of the American craft brewing community: "We are doing every kind of beer you can think of and some kinds that haven't been thought of yet, and we're having fun at it. And we're getting a lot of people to do it, and a lot more to drink it. I think that's important." Papazian became nostalgic and sentimental: "Being together with Fred Eckhardt, Fritz Maytag and Ken Grossman for four hours and talk over a casual beer was an experience I've always dreamed of having." (As a result of a near-fatal car accident in 2009, Jack McCauliffe was not able to participate in the round-table discussion between the beer pioneers, but a few months later his improving health allowed him to collaborate with Ken Grossman on their barleywine beer).

For his part, Grossman was content to simply express gratitude to the people who deserved it. "We wanted to pay tribute to the original pioneers who helped me and hundreds of others get started," he said with a mix of modesty and loyalty to the craft-brewing profession—like the good captain he is.

It seemed entirely appropriate that, in return, Ken Grossman was paid one of the highest tributes by the brewing profession at the Brewers Association Annual Conference in April 2010. By winning the Russell Schehrer Award for Innovation in Brewing, he joined a small, select group of brewers honored for their groundbreaking contributions to the industry. In his nomination letter, Vinnie Cilurzo of Russian River Brewing Co. said: "Ken Grossman founded Sierra Nevada Brewing Company thirty years ago based on one principle, to make the highest quality beer in America. ... I think Ken's never-ending quest in life is to make Sierra Nevada's beers even better than they already are."

Perhaps it's this quixotic quality of Ken Grossman's quest that explains why, years from now, many people will surely look back at the date November 15, 2010, and say, "I was part of the celebration; I raised my glass to toast the thirty-year milestone of one of the nation's leading craft breweries."

Scenes from the Taproom, Part IV
March 5, 2010: The Launching of Mersey Cream Stout

"Hiya Rob, howzit?" the telephone message begins. "This is Alan Judge. Listen, just wanted to tell youse that 'ave brewed a batch of Mersey Cream Stout at the Pilot Brewery. Should be racked by the end of the week. So, if youse can make it to the pub on Friday around 5:00, I'll buy yer a pint. Oh, and 'ave asked some of the lads to come along. Hope to see you there. Cheers then."

How could I refuse? It's yet another opportunity for some valuable book-research, I tell myself.

I arrive early in order to secure a seat at the Taproom bar. On a typical Friday afternoon, the place is heaving by 5:00 P.M. So I arrive at 4.30 p.m. and grab one of the few empty stools at the bar. I order a pint of Alan's Mersey Cream Stout—the name now emblazoned on one of the sixteen beer taps in front of me along with other offerings, Pale Ale, Best Bitter, Kellerweis, Stout, and a Beer Camp special called Baltic Porter.

Mersey Cream Stout is a low alcohol beer defined by sweet malt and chocolate flavors, based on a recipe that was popular when Alan and I were growing up in England in the 1960s: Mackeson's Stout. It was originally brewed by Whitbread and Company (now owned by InBev—yet another victim to a recent corporate merger). It's a classic session beer containing lactose sugar derived from milk, adding sweetness and calories to the beer not to mention nutritional value.

The man to my right is intrigued by the liquid food I am drinking. His name is Lance. Several years ago, he suffered a massive heart attack which forced him to stop working. Now, he pays a daily visit to the Taproom for a ritual pint. He's under strict doctor's orders not to exceed his daily dosage. He's on a first-name basis with Jessica, the waitress, and a few of the regulars around me. He prefers hoppy beers, he tells me, but he's impressed by the sample of Alan's stout, even if it means breaking his doctor's rules just this once.

In walks Alan. "Ay ay!" he greets me. He is wearing that look of pride again. This is his day, after all. We're here to celebrate the launching of his Mersey Stout and it's as if all of Liverpool is watching and wishing him well. I want to hear more of the story about the brewing of the beer.

He tells me: "I ran the idea by Steve Dresler a few years ago and he was immediately hooked. He said we would give it a shot at the Pilot Brewery when time allowed."

"How did you react?"

"I was stunned when he came up to me later and said I had the green light. He was excited. I thought he had forgotten about the whole thing."

"So what's special about Mersey Cream?"

"It's nothing like a typical Sierra product, not a hop bomb, not high in alcohol. Plus, the history behind this beer is romantic."

Romantic? Now, that's an interesting angle, I think to myself. Behind Alan's laddish exterior, there's clearly a soft spot. "Go on."

He tells me it came about as a throwback to his childhood memories on Merseyside, and his mother, Kathleen Judge, drinking Mackeson's during the time of rations immediately after World War II. It was advertised as "nourishing" or "sweet milk stout," he says. It was even given to nursing mothers. Popularity waned in the '70s but the style stayed alive in working class pockets such as Liverpool and Glasgow, along with "Sweetheart Stout" and "Jamaican Dragon Stout."

I'm impressed by Alan's historical knowledge of the beer style he's brewing. "Did you encounter some challenges?" I ask.

"The only real problem was using the lactose sugar, derived from milk, to prime. It is unfermentable by beer yeast but adds sweetness body and calories to the finished beer. Never having used it before, it was a taste as you go process till I finally said, 'Yes, that's it!'"

It's beginning to sound like a veritable Willy Wonka experience. "How often does an employee get the opportunity to make their own batch in the Pilot?" I wonder.

"Well, there's Beer Camp every two weeks or so. That's when we bring in invited guests from the beverage industry and set them loose in the pilot. That's been really popular and a great success. As for employees, every so often, someone will come up with an idea and then pitch it to Steve Dresler and Scott Jennings. That's how we came up with Scotch Ale and Ruthless."

"How much hands-on brewing did you get for Mersey Stout?"

"The whole kit and caboodle," he smiles. "From getting the malt up, digging out the hops, to putting the lactose in. From grain to glass."

"That's as good as it gets, Alan, eh? Stout fellow!" I can't resist the terrible pun.

We clink glasses and partake of the hallowed beverage which does not disappoint.

"Cheers!"

Then the lads arrive.

The lads are a tight-knit group of predominantly British expatriates who use beer as a vehicle for collectively indulging in nostalgia for their mythical homeland. In addition to Alan, there's Irish Cal, Scottish Murray, Italian-Anglo Elio, South African "Farmer," and Paul from London. There are also two Americans in the group, Mark and

Rick, who serve as honorary members and, as needed, peacemakers should things turn ugly, which they invariably do after a few drinks. I consider myself as an insider-outsider in the group, having lived most of my life in the U.S. but with many family members still living in England.

At some stage during these beer sessions, there's a particular topic of discussion that never fails to surface. I call it "the sacred list," essentially a roll call of the most important twosomes in the annals of human history, all of them British of course. Topping the list are luminaries like Lennon and McCartney, Morecambe and Wise, Crosse and Blackwell, Hurst and Peters, Posh and Becks. Even though any non-Brit listening into the conversation would have no idea who most of these cultural icons are (nor, to be perfectly honest, should they really care), we press on with our banter as if we're debating the most important topic on the planet. Before long, we're moaning about the miserable weather back home, lamenting the lack of pork pies and Typhoo tea in Chico, and debating who was the greatest comedian in the history of television—Benny Hill or Ken Dodd.

Thus we lapse into our predictable spate of nostalgia, fueled by rounds of Alan's Mersey Stout.

"Did you know that Mersey Stout is a version of Mackeson's that we used to have back home?" I point out.

Elio perks up. "Remember that TV advertisement for Mackeson's back in the '60s?"

A chorus of voices bursts into "Ah Mackeson's! Looks good, tastes good, and by golly, it does you good!"

Dutifully, we take it in turns to repeat the jingle over and over—on each occasion trying to perfect the distinctive vowels and consonants of the actor in the commercial. His name was Bernard Miles: he had a lush, bass-baritone voice, the embodiment of the proper English country gentleman.

We're in full flow by now and we quickly move on to a memory game of the most famous beer jingles that we can dredge up from the past.

"Double Diamond Works Wonders!"

"Guinness is Good for You."

"Heineken Refreshes the Parts Other Beers Cannot Reach."

Then we start recalling other famous advertising slogans from our misty childhoods.

"Ah, Bisto"

"Don't forget the fruit gums, Mum"

"Polo, the mint with the hole"

Sure enough, after a few more drinks, we approach a topic that British expatriates around the world regularly address with unfailing intensity: why England has never won the World Cup soccer tournament for the last fifty years. If you ask the lads to name England's finest hour, chances are they won't mention Winston Churchill or Dunkirk in June 1940; rather, they'll jabber on about Bobby Moore lifting the Jules Rimet trophy in Wembley Stadium on July 30, 1966. After all, it's our right to win the World Cup every four years, surely. Why we haven't done so needs to be examined thoroughly, preferably over a few drinks. So we probe the mystery further.

"Well, we're no good at penalty kicks," Elio says. "That's the bottom-line."

"There's a reason for that, you know," Farmer chimes in. "The whole world is against England. That's why we never win with penalty kicks. It's a conspiracy."

"I think it's the lack of mid-field penetration," Cal says thoughtfully. "Paul Gascoigne—now there was a player with quick feet and good ball control."

"Bloody rubbish, mate," Murray scoffs. "Look at him now—a basket-case."

"Our long-ball tactics are a joke," Paul says. "We should play more like Arsenal. Now there's a team that can pass the ball."

"Let's face it, we're bloody shite," Alan says with particular fervor.

In scouse-talk, this is called *"avin" a bit of a barney*. For the most part, the banter is all good fun. But the threat of verbal and physical violence is never far away and all it takes is one stray comment for things to turn nasty.

It's at times like this when Mark—aware of the delicate situation at hand—plays his Woodrow Wilson hand: "Well, I think it's great to watch England play. I mean—'Three lions on a shirt.' Wow, I love this team and the pride they show."

Suddenly, the mood changes. All is bright and beautiful once again now that patriotic pride is restored. "There you go, son," Elio proclaims approvingly. "'Three lions on a shirt.' Now that's what I'm talking about."

It seems we're about to lapse into a recital of "We few, we happy few, we band of brothers," but Farmer quickly changes the subject. "Hey Alan," he says. "How many barrels of this stuff did you make?"

"Fifteen."

"Oh well. That should be enough to keep us going for tonight then, eh?"

On that note, it's time for me to leave. I don't have the same staying power as my compatriots. No doubt they will close the place down, as they usually do. But it has been another memorable session at the pub. Thanks to this exalted beer brewed in my adopted country, I've enjoyed another evening of unabashed nostalgia for my ancestral homeland across the pond.

CHAPTER FIVE

Hop Harmony at Work: Sierra Nevada and the Triple P (People, Planet, Profit)

NARRATIVES OF HOPE

MOST READERS will undoubtedly agree that the recent financial meltdown has been devastating and disconcerting. In 2008 alone, $1.7 trillion dollars of wealth was wiped off the map. A new vocabulary of fraud, deception, and unregulated risk-taking surfaced, spawning words and phrases like derivatives, CDOs (collaterized debt obligations) toxic assets, tranches, and Ponzi schemes. The prevailing mandate for running a business seemed to go something like this: cut costs of production by any means possible, raise salaries and bonuses for top management, and maximize profits for owners and investors. It's not only the predominant business model that is in crisis. We also face chronic challenges from an ongoing threat of climate change coupled with an increasingly rapid depletion of natural resources such as clean air, water, even fossil fuels.

Thankfully, not everyone is pessimistic in the face of these challenges. An assortment of activists, grassroots campaigners, and ethical businesses has emphatically restated the importance of simply "doing the right thing." In his book, *Blessed Unrest: How the Largest Movement in the World Came into Being and Why No One Saw It Coming,* Paul Hawken asserts the need for "narratives of imagina-

tion and conviction, not defeatist accounts about [our] limits" (4).
He sets out to examine extraordinary people and institutions that
have made a difference to the quality of life on the planet—not
just businesses but also philosophers, politicians, entrepreneurs,
poets, spiritual guides, activists. They constitute, he argues, "the
largest social movement in all of human history" (4). They are dis-
parate voices, not necessarily organized into one bloc nor situated
in the same hemisphere; but they all work with a similar vision
and end result in mind. What they have in common, he says, is
that they care passionately about fostering the quality of life. He
singles out various places and institutions that support such noble
goals: "universities, temples, poetry, choirs, parks, literature, language, museums, terraced fields, long marriages, line dancing,
and art" (134). They are worthy of preservation, he argues. The
list is seemingly random and every reader will probably want to
add their favorite institution to the list.

I propose to add brewpub or pub to this list: places where
ideas and laughter can be shared freely, where the inner workings
of the mind are fired by a magical libation and inspired by comfortable external surroundings. I heartily agree with the British
beer writer, Michael Jackson, when he says, "Proper pubs are ha-
vens in which one can anchor the soul, and hope. They have pockets of peace and conversational corners. They offer the possibility
to think-and-drink or talk-and-drink." As Hawken puts it, places
like these are "What makes life worthwhile and enables civilization to endure" (134).

Ironically, while pubs are facing a serious decline in my country of birth, Britain, closing at an alarming rate, the rising popularity of craft breweries and pubs or brewpubs in my adopted
homeland provides a distinctive American twist to a centuries-old
tradition of beer culture. Many of these craft breweries have in
the last decade subscribed to progressive economic, environmental, and social agendas. That makes them ideal institutions to examine as exemplars of hope and good governance. And primary

among these is Sierra Nevada Brewing Co.

WHEN GOWN MEETS TOWN

I N THE three-year course of writing and researching this book, as the global economy tanked and domestic unemployment rates spiked, as the planet continued to endure a succession of environmental catastrophes, I became intrigued by a recurring question: What lessons can be learned from the success story of Sierra Nevada? The company has weathered the recession well. Its repertoire of beer continues to garner rave reviews universally. Workers at the company are demonstrably happy and fulfilled. Its sustainability agenda wins top honors and awards with predictable regularity. And the company's brand has earned a fiercely loyal following. Surely, there's something of value to take away from this. If nothing else, the company's success offers a welcome antidote to the gloom and despair pervading the current zeitgeist.

Often, in the past three years, I would leave my university campus—where morale has been weakened by furloughs, ceaseless budget cuts, and out-of-control class sizes—and drive across Chico to the brewery to be met by friendly receptionists and laid-back yet business-like professionals. With pride, they would show me around the sparkling clean facilities; with patience, they would explain the issue I was investigating; and with considerable passion, they would explicate the business of making and selling good beer. This upbeat mood contrasted starkly with the despondency of the institution that I had left behind. Make no mistake: I love my teaching job and I am grateful for the opportunities that academia has provided me, none more so than the perpetual challenge of engaging young, idealistic minds in the art of dialogue. I've spent most of my life since the age of eighteen ensconced in some kind of ivory tower—studying or teaching in a college campus setting. Whenever I travel, I always try to make a beeline to the nearest university and enjoy the special vibe uniquely offered

by learning communities worldwide. If there's a pub or bar nearby, then so much the better because it's often the perfect vantage-
point from which to explore the disputes as well as the dynamic
interactions that characterize local town-gown relations.

As I continued to work on this book, I soon became aware
that I was experiencing another kind of dialogue—one that went
beyond the confines of my classroom. I became fascinated by the
recurring question: What can my university learn from Sierra Nevada? In particular, what can the brewery teach us about the world
we live in, whether we're trying to learn how to run a flourishing
business or simply how to live a good life? In short, what can be
gained from Sierra Nevada's mantra, "Hop harmony"?

My purpose here is not to evaluate the relative effectiveness of
different business models such as the family-owned business model versus the state-owned business model or the corporate business model. The strengths and limitations of these models have
been analyzed in detail elsewhere. Rather, I wish to share what I
have observed at Sierra Nevada these past thirty-six months and
why I think there are many universal lessons to be learned from
the company's evolving philosophy. It has been an education for
me, luring me away from my ivory tower, exposing me to a "real
world" business model that is exciting, inspiring, and—as I will
suggest—a bearer of genuine hope.

THE TRIPLE P

"GREED IS good," vaunted Michael Douglas in the 1987
film *Wall Street*, echoing the values of high-stakes
businessmen such as Ivan Boesky and Michael
Milken who at the time broke the law repeatedly, seduced by the
mandate of a singular bottom line: the need to make a profit,
no matter the cost to human or environmental health. A quarter
of a century later, businesses still depend on turning a profit, of
course, but nowadays a more expansive business model is preva-

lent, one that, at the very least, satisfies its employees and customers by treating them with respect and that is attentive to the
needs and demands of the environment.

One of the most prominent of these models is the "triple bottom line," a phrase coined by social entrepreneur, John Elkington,
in 1994 to apply to businesses with the subheading descriptors,
"People, Planet, Profit." His purpose was to broaden the discussion of sustainability to address economic and social concerns,
not just ecological matters. In 2007, the "triple bottom line" was
adopted by the United Nations as a blueprint for businesses to
follow in order to expend natural and human capital wisely and
ethically.

The new paradigm, therefore, fosters economic, ecological,
and social benefits in an interlocking matrix. It's called "eco-effi-
ciency," combining equity, ecology, and economy. It blends commerce and the commonweal. Elkington went on to contribute
to the formulation of a Global Reporting Initiative (GRI) which
was conceived with a set of guidelines to help companies measure and monitor their sustainability performance. The GRI was
organized into a worldwide network of institutions that tracked
performances in six categories: environment, human rights, labor
practices and decent work, society, product responsibility, and
economy.

This new paradigm can be summed up by one trenchant question: How to be a part of the solution to the world's environmental and social problems, not the problem itself? Andrew Savitz is
a consultant for sustainable business strategies. He works with a
range of organizations, from Fortune 100 companies to major
nonprofits. In his book *The Triple Bottom Line: How Today's Best-Run
Companies Are Achieving Economic, Social, and Environmental Success—
And How You Can Too,* Savitz argues that becoming a sustainable enterprise "entails making a shift from an old way of thinking to a
new one—a new mind-set that subtly or dramatically alters everything you see and do" (227).

In this chapter, I outline Sierra Nevada's distinctive method of applying the triple bottom line. After all, as Savitz says: "We want to be living together here on planet Earth for a long time, and to do so, we will eventually have to change our way of looking at things" (234).

People

The Global Reporting Initiative covers not only fair and just labor practices at the workplace but also, more broadly, the impact of the company on the local community and society at large; in particular, the value of the product and its harmful or helpful contributions to the welfare of consumers.

If loyalty to a company and low turnover rates of its workforce are criteria for judging an effective business, then Sierra Nevada Brewing Co. sets a model example. Around Chico, it's a well-known fact that the brewery is a great place to work. This isn't simply because it pays its workers above the state's hourly minimum wage, but also because of the variety of employee-appreciation perks that come with the job: beer bucks with every paycheck (worth a case of beer), "Lunch with the chief" (whereby Ken Grossman invites a selected employee to lunch at his or her favorite restaurant around town), "Brewer for a Day" (granting a hands-on brewing experience for the lucky worker), birthday cake (for that special day), free t-shirts, even mustard and beef giveaways (when supplies permit). This is not to mention the open invitation extended to all workers and family-members to attend the annual Christmas holiday party in the Big Room.

Carrie Alden, director of human resources, goes down this list of perks with me. She can't suppress giggles of mirth and merriment during our interview. I'm not sure whether this is because of the natural high spirits and passion she feels for her job, or because as she talks she's being distracted by a bobblehead of Ken Grossman with a Superman body that sits on the desk between us. At any rate, her fun-loving humor and zest seem emblematic of the company.

What's her secret to keeping workers happy and fulfilled? Out comes another list; this time, it's her secret formula for increasing the engagement of the company's employees: "Know them. Grow them. Inspire them. Involve them. Reward them."

As Grossman tells me later: "Part of our success has come from making people want to come to work and be proud about the workplace. The level of job satisfaction goes hand in hand with pride at what you do. We try to make it a good, fun workplace. And I have a lot of workers who tell me they wake up happy to come to work. That's the goal!" The result is a stable, productive, and contented workforce with an overall retention rate of 82 percent. The majority of these employees (around 350) work locally while about a hundred are employed as sales representatives and drivers outside Chico.

The goal of Sierra Nevada's benefits structure is to promote health, happiness, and long-term financial security. Employees have 5 percent of their annual total gross compensation automatically channeled into a profit share plan retirement program; if, in addition, they elect to defer 10 percent of their paycheck to the 401(k) plan, then a matching 10 percent sum is added by the company. Insurance premiums for a self-funded group health plan are subsidized over 80 percent by the company.

Oasis is an on-site medical clinic and wellness program where employees and immediate family members have free access to a range of healthcare services such as consulting with a physician's assistant or nurse practitioner, treating minor conditions (from allergy relief to curbing excess alcohol consumption), a free massage therapy or reflexology treatment every three months, and developing strategies for stress management. Grossman observes: "Long term, it saves us money. Absenteeism is lower, and the health of our employees is better. We've literally saved some people's lives who previously did not want to go to see a doctor.

But now they can go over (to the Oasis) for free, six days a week."

In order to encourage proactive health management, a Healthy Opportunity Program (HOP) provides resources for helping employees attain optimal health in four overlapping categories: physical, emotional, intellectual, and social. At the end of every year, active participants in this program are rewarded with "Hoppy" prizes in the form of gift certificates.

Further benefits have been added recently, including a childcare center, Little Foot (which takes in children from six months to six years old), an organic garden where employees are encouraged to grow their own food, and a transportation subsidy program, Green Machine (which offers incentives for employees to bike, car pool, or take the bus to work).

In the belief that health and happiness often derive from altruistic behavior, Sierra Nevada encourages employees to participate in community-based volunteer programs such as park and highway cleanups, Relay for Life, Bowl for Kids' Sake, Memory Walk for Alzheimer's, and regular blood drives. It has been a longstanding donor to local schools and universities, not to mention the local public radio station. In fact, if you're driving through the North State, sooner or later you're likely to hear a public radio announcer thanking Sierra Nevada Brewing Co. for its ongoing support of the station.

Despite being a midsized craft brewery, and one of the largest employers in the city of Chico, the company still holds on to a flat management structure as opposed to the deep vertical hierarchies of larger, corporate organizations. In other words, there are fewer levels between the executive level and frontline employees. This results in a "Go to Ken" mantra which I frequently observed during my visits. "Is there a problem?" someone might ask and the answer inevitably would be, "Go to Ken. He can fix it." The advantage of the flat structure is that it encourages more participation from employees and allows quick, efficient access to the top when difficult decisions need to be made. The main disadvantage is that it puts more weight and responsibility on the CEO.

When I sit down with Bill Bales, chief financial officer, he takes out a pen and starts to draw a flow diagram to help me understand the company's organization. Ken's box is at the top, then he draws a second tier of eight empty boxes representing senior managers. As he starts to fill the boxes with departments and names "Al—plant manager," "Carrie—human resources," "Steve—brewery," he wavers and gives up.

"You'll have to ask Ken," he says, finally. "He can tell you."

I share this anecdote not to suggest that Sierra Nevada's chief financial officer is incompetent (far from it, he's one of the most level-headed, laid-back businessmen I've met) nor to indicate that the company is totally dependent on Ken Grossman's decision-making; rather, my purpose is to illustrate the wide respect shown towards Grossman's business intelligence as much as his brewing genius.

Planet

In 1991, a Belgian businessman, Gunter Pauli, launched a Zero Emissions Concept, later adopted as a formal business initiative by the United Nations. The future challenge for humanity, according to Pauli, was to create businesses that could run entirely on clean, renewable energy. Given the high demand of water, heat, and cooling involved in the various stages of the brewing process, Pauli's challenge would appear as impossible as trying to square the circle, for a brewery at least. Yet Sierra Nevada—along with other notable examples such as Mad River Brewing Company in Blue Lake (Arcata, California), and New Belgium Brewing Company in Fort Collins, Colorado—has risen to the challenge.

In chapter four, I described in detail how Sierra Nevada's agenda of sustainability and stewardship intensified and modernized over time. Here, I wish to examine the company's green credentials by focusing on four specific performance indicators: air quality, water quality, energy usage, and waste products.

Carbon dioxide and methane gases are natural by-products of the brewing process. Without a successful intervention strategy, the harmful impact of these gases would be far-reaching. At Sierra Nevada, the carbon dioxide that is released during fermentation is captured by a recovery plant, then purified, stored, and reused primarily as carbonation for the bottling process. Methane is similarly captured and used to fuel the boilers.

(There's another dimension to this topic of air quality. On a crisp, cool morning as I'm biking to campus through Lower Bidwell Park, a potent smell of roasting malt blows over town from the brewery a couple of miles away and it mixes with the sharp scents of autumn to trigger powerful memories and fond reminiscences of hot porridge breakfasts taken in a deep English winter).

Water is a precious commodity, particularly in California. A brewery, on average, uses five gallons of water to produce one gallon of beer. Sierra Nevada's wastewater treatment facility, consisting of a two-stage anaerobic/aerobic digester, removes more than 95 percent of unwanted materials from the brewery's wastewater before it is released safely back into the municipal sewer system or used to drip irrigate the nine-acre estate hop field. Since 2009, Sierra Nevada has partnered with Western Rivers Conservancy to protect major rivers in the West such as the Feather, Smith, and Snake by conserving land alongside the rivers and keeping waterways clean.

As for energy, the key question remains: Is it possible to have a zero carbon footprint? Is it possible to delink from the electricity grid and become entirely self-supporting? Even though this may be practically unobtainable for a brewery, the goal is still worthwhile to pursue. A combination of solar and fuel cell energy generates close to 90 percent of Sierra Nevada's on-site energy needs. On bright sunny days, it is able to return power to the grid. And in emergencies—such as during the winter storm of 2008 or a possible summer heat wave—it can decouple from the grid altogether.

What about waste? Sierra Nevada regularly diverts an average of 99.6 percent of its solid waste material from the local landfill. In addition to spent yeast, hops, malt, and water, other peripherals are resourcefully recycled: wood pallets, glass bottles, stretch wrap, burlap packaging, office paper, light bulbs, computers, construction materials, even coffee grounds.

As a result of these initiatives, the brewery has been recognized by state agencies such as the California Integrated Waste Management Program and the California Resource Recovery Association for its waste reduction strategies. It participates in the California Climate Action Registry that measures greenhouse gas emissions, reporting daily emissions on its website.

Even if it's impossible to achieve the goal of becoming an entirely zero carbon footprint brewery, Sierra Nevada will always strive to come close at every stage of the manufacturing supply chain—from the harnessing of raw materials and supplies, through the actual brewing process, to the proper disposal of waste. For this reason, *Food Engineering* magazine recognized Sierra Nevada Brewing Co. as Sustainable Plant of the Year in 2009.

Profit

The free-market economist, Milton Friedman, once said: "There is one and only one social responsibility of business—to use its resources and engage in activities designed to increase its profits so long as it stays within the rules of the game." What rules? Clearly, the recent Wall Street fallout indicates that rules are either broken with impunity or simply ignored. In his book *The Corporation* (2004), Joel Bakan claims that corporations suffer from "a pathological pursuit" of profit and power. He argues that they are "deliberately programmed, indeed legally compelled, to externalize costs without regard for the harm [they] may cause to people, communities, and the natural environment" (72–73).

At Sierra Nevada, the concept of profit is connected to the broader notion of value. Rather than focus on short-term monetary gains, the ethos of the company seems to be guided by a different profit motive: an increase in the value of social capital, cultural capital, community capital, and environmental capital. As Bill Bales, the company's chief financial officer, points out to me, doing the right thing is wired into Sierra Nevada's DNA. "It's our responsibility to give back to the community," he says. "In most organizations, benevolence is tied to marketing in the form of sponsorships. But in our particular case, we're not publicly traded so we're not trying to appease shareholders. We tend to focus on giving back because it is simply the 'right thing to do.'" Among the beneficiaries of this altruistic form of giving are Chico State, UC Davis, Enloe Hospital, Salvation Army, the Western Rivers Conservancy, and National Public Radio.

As a privately owned company, Sierra Nevada is not obliged to disclose its revenue performance; nevertheless, some of its financial figures are public knowledge. For the fiscal year, 2008–2009, the brewery was the biggest business contributor to Chico city property taxes by a factor of three over any other business, paying more than $1 million. It has an average annual payroll of around $10 million which mostly stays in the local economy and it enjoys average annual sales of around $150 million.

Sierra Nevada's progressive waste management practices offer a vivid example of how the value of social capital, cultural capital, community capital, and environmental capital can be increased while still helping to preserve higher profit margins. By diverting over 30,000 tons of waste, the company not only helps keep the local landfill from growing unhealthily, but it also saves $4.7 million in tipping fees. In turn, this extra revenue can then be used to improve employee benefits, upgrade equipment infrastructure, or fund philanthropic projects.

As Bill Bales says: "We're not greedy. It's not all about greed and profitability."

TEN DEFINING BUSINESS PRACTICES

V ALUABLE AS the idea behind the triple bottom line may be, sometimes it's also necessary to look beyond the slogan. That is my intention in the following section where I cull from interviews, company documents, and media reports to draw up a list of ten business practices that, I believe, define Sierra Nevada.

The Long-Term View

Ken Grossman believes that "the long view is lacking in the policy decisions of many companies." Installing cutting-edge technologies requires an investment that may not provide short-term payback for at least several years as exemplified by the purchase of the solar array, the fuel cells, and the carbon dioxide capture plant. Freed of shareholder pressure for quick profits, Grossman can focus on what he considers the right thing to do. "We are now at a size where these technologies are affordable," he concedes. A company the size of Sierra Nevada is able to recycle its profits into larger capital projects with a payback time that is often too long for a smaller company to afford.

Closing the Loop

Instead of an industrial process governed by a cradle to grave model (in which waste by-products end up on ever-expanding landfills), cradle to cradle is a more sustainable paradigm. Closing the loop is a circular rather than linear model that aims to eliminate the concept of waste by recycling all materials in the supply chain.

How do you close the loop?

When, in early 2009, I present this question to Cheri Chastain, Sierra Nevada's sustainability coordinator, she replies by using the brewery's nine-acre hop field as an example. Her explanation is worth quoting in full: "We've got the hop field on site. We're using compost that's made from our by-products. So we've got organics leaving our process producing compost that then goes onto the hop field to grow the hops. Starting this spring, we'll be recycling treated wastewater back on to the hop field to irrigate it. So we've got two things leaving our process, water and the organics, which we can recycle back on to the hop field. We then harvest those hops, brewing them for the Chico Estate Harvest Beer, all the while recycling steam for the brewing process, recycling the heat and the cold. And then we're producing vegetable oil out of the restaurant where people go to have their Chico Estate Harvest Beer along with some fries; the vegetable oil that's leaving the restaurant produces a biodiesel fuel that goes into the vehicles that we're using to deliver the beer that was brewed with hops that were grown from recycled water and compost. That's probably one of my favorite closed loops, and it covers upstream as well as downstream. I really like that one!"

Quality Assurance

Quality has always been a predominant principle at Sierra Nevada. It is even enshrined in the original Business Plan of 1979 which proclaims, "The quality (of beer) must be high and have good taste." It still predominates today, thirty years later. Says Grossman: "We've not altered our brewing approach one bit but what we have done is improved the consistency. I've still got my original recipe for Pale Ale and it's pretty much identical to the beer that's brewed today."

Rob Fraser, head of quality control, describes the philosophy as "quality over cost." He cites the example of the company's change from using twist-off caps to pry-offs. It was a costly decision: there was much negative press from consumers, not to mention a wholesale restructuring of the entire bottling line. But it was the right thing to do for the quality of beer.

Stewardship

Traditionally, the word "steward" has meant many things, from God's agent on Earth to the manager of property or household affairs. More recently, it has acquired another resonance: guardian of the land and environment. Ken Grossman sees himself not just as a brewer or businessman but also as a steward in the broader sense, concerned as much about his company's carbon footprint as the quality of his beer and quality of life in the community he inhabits. While hiking the Sierra Nevada range one summer, the naturalist John Muir observed, "When we try to pick out anything by itself, we find it hitched to everything else in the universe." Ken Grossman likes to walk that talk.

Minimization and Optimization

According to Andrew Savitz, this is "the sweet spot where sustainability and profitability meet" (104). Minimization means "reducing the size of your footprint, in terms of the adverse environmental, social, and economic impacts of your activities" (151). Once a business starts to minimize its harmful impact, he argues, the process of optimization ("being more good") automatically kicks in. According to Savitz, "Optimization aims not just to reduce pollution, but to restore the environment; not just to eliminate employee accidents, but to create a healthier, happier workforce; not just to decrease harm to the community, but to revitalize it" (151).

The principle of minimization encourages a business to: reduce workplace accidents, clean up hazardous wastes, reduce the use of fossil fuels, reduce the use of needless packaging, and respond quickly to customer complaints. At the same time, by observing the principle of optimization, a business is encouraged to: create a healthy and happy workforce, use waste as feedstock for other products, use green power, use biodegradable packaging, learn from complaints to make new and better products.

Management Triage

The concept of triage typically applies to the medical profession. For example, in an attempt to make the most efficient use of available resources, hospital emergency rooms routinely establish a priority procedure for treating patients according to need and expediency. Hal Johnson, chairman of the consulting firm Leadership One, defines management triage as "the assigning of priority order to projects on the basis of where funds and resources can best be used to achieve your vision." In 2006, he completed a study of several companies that had quickly expanded beyond their early startup status. As they grew, he noticed that they would often lose their founding vision, adding layers of middle management to their operating structure. Not so Sierra Nevada Brewing Co., according to Johnson: "They have done an incredible job of identifying the most important things to do—as well as not to do."

When I ask Ken Grossman for his company's mission statement, he hands me a short one-page document that identifies core values:

Quality: "Our products and services should exceed peoples' expectations."

Integrity: "We develop relationships where people trust and respect us."

People: "We greatly value and are fully committed to our employees."

Community: "We respect and support the community in which we live."

Sustainability: "We work smartly and efficiently so we can continue to prosper."

One reason for the effectiveness of Sierra Nevada's management is the flat organizational structure of the company. Few levels of hierarchy separate Ken Grossman from his staff (as opposed to large corporate structures where layers of middle management often separate the top from bottom). Says Gil Sanchez (director of research and development): "We're always striving to further eliminate barriers to communication. Having only a few levels of management allows us to respond more quickly and efficiently to changing business needs and opportunities, and I expect it also improves employee exposure, sense of value, and satisfaction."

Bioregionalism

"Could beer save the world?" That's the question posed recently in an article published in *The Guardian* from London. The answer given is: emphatically yes. Beer is at the center of a green revolution, argues the author: "Brewers are using small-scale technologies, developing local markets, reducing packaging and shipping, making use of locally available materials, and reducing overall waste through eco-industrial design." This is the embodiment of bioregionalism, he claims, and it helps to explain the increasing appeal of local breweries with their strong regional identities.

Sierra Nevada's Harvest Estate Ale, for example, advances the concepts of "terroir" and "provenance." It is truly a local ale, using crops grown in Sierra Nevada's own hop and barley fields. The locavore movement, founded in Berkeley in 2005, challenged consumers in the Bay Area to eat food produced within a hundred-mile radius of their home for a month. Barbara Kingsolver extends the challenge to a whole year in her memoir, *Animal, Vegetable, Miracle* (2007). Locally grown produce not only offers social and environmental advantages, it also provides added pleasure by fostering connections, responsibility, and loyalty to the region. As Kingsolver admits: "We hoped a year away from industrial foods would taste so good, we might actually enjoy it" (22).

Stakeholders Over Shareholders

The term "stakeholder," according to Andrew Savitz, was first introduced by Professor R. Edward Freeman in 1984 to refer to "anyone who is affected by, or can affect an organization" (59). It included "internal stakeholders" (such as employees), "stakeholders in your value chain" (from the supplier to customers), and "external stakeholders" (ranging from the media to future generations impacted by the company). Publicly-traded corporations, on the other hand, have an overriding mandate to serve the financial interests of shareholders.

As a private company, Sierra Nevada Brewing Co. is not answerable to shareholders. Yet, as indicated in chapter three, there were several opportunities for the company to be floated on the stock exchange, especially during the late 1990s. Other brewing companies, notably Boston Beer Company, followed the strategy of satisfying investors' needs for short-term returns and high yielding dividends. (In defense of shareholding, investors have an active interest in the welfare of the company and can, in theory at least, influence the company's decision-making process).

When it comes to stakeholder mapping, who are the company's stakeholders? The answer, I discover, ranges from the employee to the consumer. "Engagement, empathy, and profitability" are the values emphasized by Carrie Alden, human resources officer at Sierra Nevada. "We're wired to care," she says.

Health and Happiness

Beer is a form of "liquid bread," highly nutritious, high in fiber, low in fat and cholesterol. (The much maligned beer belly comes from the unhealthy food that often accompanies excessive beer drinking). Beer is good with food pairings and when cooking food such as chili, stew, steaks, and burgers. It's good for the garden as plant food or fertilizer. For many, it stimulates health and happiness. Earlier in the book, I quoted Benjamin Franklin on beer: "Beer is living proof that God loves us and wants us to be happy." Whether or not he actually spoke these words is the subject of an ongoing historical debate and need not concern us here. What's important is the core truth expressed in the quote. It's no coincidence that beer is often referred to as the liquid of the gods or as a divine nectar. The reason is surely because of its magical transformative properties capable of producing considerable pleasure.

As Samuel Johnson wisely said: "There is nothing which has yet been contrived by man, by which so much happiness is produced as by a good tavern or inn."

The Pleasure Principle

It doesn't take a Freudian psychoanalyst to realize that "the pleasure principle" can be both delightful and dangerous at the same time. I certainly don't want my argument to be misunderstood here. I am not advocating mindless nor excessive consumption of beer, or any alcoholic drink for that matter. Binge drinking and lager loutishness run counter to the spirit of this book and I do not condone these practices. But I do believe there is a middle way: a tasteful, moderate method of gaining joy and pleasure from the aid of a liquid that enacts subtle changes on the mind, inducing states of euphoria and bliss. Mark Youngquist, the head brewer of Dolores River Brewery says it best: "I just want to drink a beer that subtly reminds me, with every sip, how lucky I am to be alive, surrounded by beauty and good people, and living right here, right now."

This is what, I believe, is ultimately meant by Hop Harmony—it's not just looking after people, planet, and profits; it's also a way of giving pleasure and tapping into the fundamental human spirit, what Greek philosophers used to call "eudaimonia" or human flourishing.

The Sierra Nevada Brewing Co. family (all employees), 2010

Scenes from the Taproom, Part V
March 31, 2010: The Answers to Life's Really Big Questions

It's Cesar Chavez Day, a university holiday. I decide to spend a few hours working on the book in my campus office before heading over to Sierra Nevada for an afternoon drink and chat with Jim and Jessica Mellem, one of several couples who work at the brewery. I have questions about the role of women in the brewing industry and the quality of Chico's water. Jim and Jessica are the go-to people for these topics, I've been told.

At around 9:00 A.M., I park my car in a student neighborhood southwest of the Chico State campus. It's a quiet morning. But by the time I leave my office in the late afternoon and return to the car, I am appalled by the transformation that has taken place: groups of students in cheap ponchos and fake sombreros are shuffling down the street, yelping in Spanglish and waving red party cups in the air. The fraternity on the opposite side of the street from where my car is parked is hosting a party in its front yard. Faux-Mexican music blares from powerful speaker amplifiers and bronzed bodies are gyrating to the repetitive beat. So this is how historical legacies get passed on, I say to myself. It feels wrong somehow. I'm not sure what they're drinking in those plastic cups, tequila or beer, but if it's Sierra Nevada I certainly won't use this as an opportunity to celebrate or glorify the product.

The scene is more muted at the brewery, a couple of miles south of campus. It's 4.00 P.M. and a row of customers is once again enjoying beer at the Taproom bar. There's no evidence of a Cesar Chavez celebration here, apart perhaps from the occasional measured toast in his honor. I take my place at the end of the bar and wait for Jim and Jessica. A middle-aged couple enters and hovers behind me. The two seem like friendly people. As it turns out, they're visiting from Pennsylvania and have come directly to the brewery from Chico Municipal Airport.

"Do you have anything like a Ying-ling?" the man asks Jessica, the waitress.

She looks bemused. "Sorry, we don't serve Chinese beers here. Only Sierra Nevada."

"Ying-ling," he persists. "It's what they brew in Pennsylvania at one of the oldest breweries in the nation. It's a nice, smooth lager."

At this point, Jim arrives. I tell him about the confusion. He jumps on the case right away. "Oh, Yuengling," he says with confident authority. "Pottsville. Great place. Great brewery. Yes, I recommend a Summerfest or Blonde Ale. They are both pleasant lagers, not too strong, but they have a nice bite to them. That's as close as you'll get to a Yuengling lager."

He proceeds to offer technical information about the difference between Sierra Nevada's yeast strains and those used at Yuengling. It's more than I can understand and probably more than the friendly gentleman from Pennsylvania needs to hear, but the man smiles kindly at Jim while waiting for his Summerfest to be poured and then moves away from the bar to join his wife, seemingly satisfied with his choice of beer.

Jim graduated in 2000 from UC Davis with a bachelor of science in food science and technology. His first job was as a part-time technician at Anheuser-Busch in Fairfield but was hired soon afterwards by Sierra Nevada where he worked in quality assurance. He quickly moved to R&D, where he conducted research into aroma and taste profiles of beer; more recently, he has been promoted to the position of cellar supervisor (in charge of fermentation, yeast handling, and dry hopping). He is also the assistant brewmaster (under Steve Dresler). Clearly, he has earned his steady promotions; he knows what he's talking about. He can be forgiven if, at times, he forgets he's talking to an ordinary layman with only a partial understanding of beer's subtleties.

I've enjoyed working with Jim. Early in my research stages, he was kind enough to invite me to attend a Friday sensory analysis taste panel. Regularly, luminaries from the brewery assemble together in the testing lab and evaluate beer samples for defects and unsavory flavors such as metallic or earthy tones. Of course, these are laymen's terms. A technician is expected to use appropriate terminology like "too much mercaptan" (rotten vegetables) or my favorite, "hint of butyric acid" (baby sick). The curious thing is that of the six beer samples I tasted on this particular Friday morning, I thought they were all pretty good! In fact, I readily finished the samples without detecting a significant fault in any of them. Then I listened to the panel of experts analyze each sample with the critical analysis of a detective. Was there something wrong with my taste buds, I wondered? Or, perhaps, I had an underdeveloped sense of beer appreciation? Once again, I was reminded that I had much to learn about beer.

Jim is a cross between Gene Wilder in *Willy Wonka and the Chocolate Factory* and Alfred E. Neuman, the poster boy for *Mad* magazine. He has a deep, barrelly voice, a quick wit, and a penetrating scientific brain. In other words, he's a perfect character for my story and a good guide for me as I work my way through the world of beer.

We're soon joined by his wife Jessica who is brimming with bright-eyed idealism on this fresh spring afternoon. She graduated from Chico State in 2001 with a degree in microbiology. She is now the supervisor of the packaging department. They married in 2008.

Jim orders a pint of Alan's Mersey Stout. I'm surprised there's still some left in the barrel. I thought the lads polished it off two weeks ago when I was here for its launch, but apparently not. Jessica orders a Torpedo IPA.

She tells me that women don't always want a weak, fizzy beer that is low in carbs and alcohol content. She's obviously got a point because, as she's talking, she sips zealously from her pint of Torpedo which at 7.2 percent ABV can be characterized as a big beer with lots of hop profile. There's an increasingly important role for women in brewing circles, she goes on to explain. The establishment of women's advocacy groups such as Pink Boots Society and Women Enjoying Beer has been crucial.

In addition, she reveres female role models like Kim Jordan, Rhonda Kallman, and Carol Stoudt—all of whom enjoy established reputations as brewery owners and brewmasters. The face of brewing is changing, Jessica says. As if to prove her point, she orders another pint of Torpedo.

The increasingly important role of women in brewing is a topic that I should continue to track for a future project, I note to myself. But I've also come here today to learn about the quality of water. It's well known that Chico is blessed with relatively clean water and lots of it. It sits on top of the Tuscan Aquifer, one of the largest underground reservoirs of water in the state, constantly being recharged by winter rain and runoffs from snow in the Sierra Nevada foothills.

I'm surprised when Jim tells me that there is no private well for Sierra Nevada. The brewery takes its water from a municipal water plant, then treats it and modifies it to suit the style of beer being made by using acids and calcium salts.

"Chico water is neither hard, nor soft, nor overly alkaline," Jim says. "In fact, it's quite benign."

So far, so good. I catch the gist of what Jim is saying. I'm thankful he hasn't gone off on one of his elaborate scientific excursions. "As brewers, we like it that way," he continues. "It's sort of like having a blank canvas. We can paint the canvas any way we want. On the other hand, if you take water from, say, Burton-on-Trent, it has extremely high levels of calcium sulfate. This creates a slightly more astringent water base that is more favorable to bring out the bitterness of the hops."

I can still just about follow the thread of Jim's argument. But then he shifts gears into technical overdrive. "What matters to us most is the effect of the water on mash pH," he says. "Higher alkalinity causes a higher mash pH, while a higher hardness (with concentrations of calcium and magnesium) creates a lower mash pH. We aim for around 5.3 or 5.4 mash pH. Mineral content is also crucial. The presence of certain mineral ions will affect flavor and character of the beer. Dark beers work better in alkaline water. Sulfate accentuates hop bitterness, as I said in the case of Burton beers. This is why our brewery is free to make both ales and lagers—we modify our water. When it comes to water quality, we value cleanliness over anything else. After all, at the end of the day, it has to be Ken-good."

"*Ken-good?*" Somehow, the phrase doesn't quite match the lofty tone of the terminology he's been firing in my direction.

"Yes, it's the mantra we try to observe here at the brewery. Things have to be 'Ken-good.'"

"What does it mean?"

"Quality, quality, quality," he quickly replies.

"Oh, I see." Then I realize it's time to raise a question that I've been eager to ask for a long time. "Jim, what on earth is flocculation?"

He chuckles. "It's the process whereby colloids coagulate in the beer to create clusters."

"Uh-huh," I nod politely.

"Now this is important," says Jim, warming to his theme. "Because if the yeast flocculates too early, then the beer becomes underattentuated. But if the yeast doesn't flocculate at all, then it leaves a cloudy and yeasty taste."

"Fascinating," I say, pretending to follow along. Jessica correctly interprets my confusion.

"So, basically, what Jim is trying to say is that flocculation allows the yeast to come together while consuming the sugar in the beer. This is why you often get deposits of yeast at the bottom of the bottle. It has flocculated downwards."

At that moment, I suddenly understand the importance of flocculation to this book. It explains why my homemade beer foamed madly out of control. It got over excited. It suffered from too much flocculation. My mind is racing now. I see all sorts of interesting connections. It's not just my homebrew that was hopelessly over-flocculated. It's also the students who transformed Cesar Chavez Day into an excuse for hedonistic excess. After all, the good life, like good beer, requires moderation and balance if it's to be savored properly. Haven't all great civilizations been teaching us this simple truth over and over? In fact, shouldn't "controlled flocculation" become another mantra to respect and observe, right up there with "making things Ken-good?"

And this is what keeps me coming back to the Taproom at Sierra Nevada. Not for the first or last time, I walk away from the brewery equipped with answers to the really big questions in life.

CONCLUSION

"A LONG STRANGE TRIP"

FOR THE past three decades, Sierra Nevada Brewing Co. has been at the forefront of a dramatic beer revolution in the United States. "What a long strange trip it's been," commented Ken Grossman at the outset of his address to the American Homebrewers Association in 2009. Fittingly, he was invited to be the keynote speaker for the annual convention of homebrewers. And fittingly, he offered a salute to his appreciative audience, recognizing that the 1979 legalization of homebrewing paved the way for a radical transformation of the domestic beer industry. On stage, he was introduced by Charlie Papazian who said of Grossman: "[he is] one of the original pioneers of the craft brewing and homebrewing community. His brewery is a symbol of what we all dream of having or have dreamt of having at one time or another."

The progression from 1980 to 2010 has been remarkable as much for Sierra Nevada Brewing Co. as for the beer scene nationwide. Consider the following contrasts: Sierra Nevada started out with two employees working from a ramshackle warehouse cobbled out of recycled dairy equipment; now it's a semi-automated brewery with state-of-the art equipment, employing close to five hundred workers, operating 24/7, and filling bottles at a rate of over 1,200 per minute. Back in 1980, a few enthusiasts across the land were doing their best to initiate a conversation about the joys of making and drinking good beer; nowadays, the increased knowledge and sophistication about beer surfaces in ubiquitous blogs, forums, discussion groups, and advocacy organizations. In 1980, American beer was the laughingstock of the world; nowadays, U.S. beers are universally respected for their extravagant boldness as well as for their uncompromising adherence to tradition.

This last fact is evidenced by a recent e-mail I received from my nephew, Matt, who lives in London, close to the upscale district of Chelsea: "Just thought I'd let you know that I had a bottle of Sierra Nevada Porter on Saturday night," he wrote. "I was at a restaurant called The Big Easy on the Kings Road. It was my birthday and I was out for a meal and thought I'd better not miss the opportunity. A lovely drop, I must say!"

"Good for you, Matt," I replied. "Glad to hear that you enjoyed a Sierra Nevada Porter just a few hundred yards away from where that brand of beer was born—on the docks of the River Thames." It seemed a perfect illustration of how the American beer revolution has helped to revive old traditions while simultaneously embracing new innovations.

At the end of her historical survey of beer in the United States, Maureen Ogle provocatively asks: "How many industries can claim to have been reinvented not by government bodies or huge corporations, but by individuals? How many industries can claim an entry bar so flexible that a guy with welding skills and a few thousand bucks can shake it up and fashion something new?" (340). Most likely, she had in mind handymen like Jack McAuliffe and Ken Grossman, largely self-taught geniuses who parlayed their passion for good beer and the good life into trailblazing businesses.

CORE VALUES

YES, IT sounds almost too good to be true and you may have noticed the absence of sensationalist melodrama in this book. You may be asking: Where are the bad guys?

Where's the tension and suspense? Where are the unpredictable twists and turns that drive Hollywood dramas or *New York Times* best sellers, even film documentaries such as the recent *Beer Wars* by Anat Baron which frames the ongoing battle between "big beer" and independent brewers as a classic David versus Goliath scenario?

The answer is that I deliberately avoided such binaries—and for good reason.

True, there have been tragedies in the story such as the unfortunate death of vice president of sales, Steve Harrison. True, there have been times of great uncertainty and anxiety such as the buyout proceedings of cofounder Paul Camusi which dragged on for several years. True, there have been business risks and gambles which could easily have backfired. Yes, there is the ongoing angst that accompanies every new batch of beer, the fear that the slightest infection to a yeast microorganism may result in the whole consignment being tossed out. Yes, there is the perennial uncertainty of annual barley and hop harvests; in 2007, for example, a perfect storm of man-made and natural circumstances combined to lower supplies dramatically, causing an exorbitant price increase for essential raw materials.

Remarkably, however, whenever I visited the brewery for one of my forty-plus interviews or on-site visits, I never once encountered trepidation about the future or ill will towards competitors; rather, I always found the place to be relaxed and quintessentially mellow. A dignified serenity seems to hang in the air, mixing naturally with the robust smell of boiling hops and roasted grains. You can see the same equanimity on the faces of the waiters and bartenders in the Taproom and Restaurant or in the demeanor of the front desk receptionists who greet visitors with friendly smiles and courtesy. I have come to realize that a widespread admiration for others in the beer business is practiced at Sierra Nevada and there's no time or tolerance for personal vendettas.

This magnanimous attitude starts at the top. As one beer

journalist observes, CEO Ken Grossman has enormous respect and affection for other brewers, particularly craft brewers, because he regards them as "compatriots in the revolution of better beer—rather than fierce competitors."

In fact, the only time I noticed a wince of discomfort on the face of Ken Grossman was when I asked about relations with Boston Beer Company, the nation's top craft brewer by volume (producing close to two million barrels a year). "They're not a craft brewer," he replied. "They're a contract brewer." The fine distinction between the two was lost on me at the time. Subsequently, I discovered that Sam Adams beer is not brewed exclusively at the Boston facility but is also brewed by other contracted companies. I decided to let the issue slide, realizing this was something of a semantic quibble in craft brewing circles much like pop music fans arguing over who was the best rock group of the 1960s British invasion: the smooth-voiced Beatles or the raunchy Rolling Stones. (I was also told emphatically on several occasions during the writing of this book that Ken Grossman enjoys an amicable relationship with Jim Koch and the Boston Beer Company.)

This professional and collegial reverence for all breweries, big and small, comes from a deep understanding of the difficulties involved in producing consistently good beer, whether it's Anheuser-Busch InBev churning out millions of barrels of Bud Light every year, or a brewpub producing modest amounts of an extreme beer that is sold exclusively on-site.

The mix of integrity and generosity seems to have permeated the company's ethos ever since its inception thirty years ago. With dedication and diligence, it has stuck unswervingly to a set of core values:

Respect for tradition and for the authenticity of craft artisanal brewing (hence the continuous use of whole hops, quality grain, and bottle conditioning).

Innovation in combining of Old and New World techniques, styles, and tastes. When you mix European malts with West Coast hops and then pitch in California yeast, you end up with what brewmaster Steve Dresler calls a "fantastic hybridization."

Passion for the simple pleasure of drinking a hearty beer. This simple pleasure masks a sophisticated business agenda of overlapping philosophies, from sustainability to maintaining a healthy working force to enjoying good community relations. In short, the company is committed to making the world a better place to live in.

Quality as enshrined in the company's original 1979 business plan: "The most important sales draw of Sierra Nevada beer will be its quality." Over thirty years later, the commitment is as strong as ever.

Consistency because, in the final analysis, that's what keeps customers coming back to a tried and tested quality product.

Of course, Sierra Nevada is not alone in heeding this heady formula of business fundamentals. There are close to fifteen hundred craft breweries currently operating in the U.S. representing a range of geographical regions and identities. Many of these breweries have successfully cultivated distinctive brand identities. Boston Beer Company's profile is one of good corporate governance rooted in patriotism; "Take Pride in Your Beer," the company's website proclaims. New Belgium Brewing Company (Fort Collins, Colorado) adopts "Follow Your Folly" as its company slogan; *having fun* is listed as one of the company's ten core values and principles. Dogfish Head Craft Brewery (Milton, Delaware) has an affinity for extreme beer and boasts an audacious motto: "Off-Centered Ales for Off-Centered People." In their own, distinctive ways, they all share respect, innovation, passion, quality, and consistency as guiding principles, comprising what Maureen Ogle calls "the most dynamic, most creative brewing industry in the world."

Sierra Nevada Brewing Co., I would argue, is the longest-serving observer of this mantra. Ironically, while American craft brewers are successfully combining Old World and New World styles to create interesting hybrid products, the fate of craft breweries in the Old World is perilous. Pubs are closing down at the rate of almost two a day in my ancestral homeland, the United Kingdom. The Village Pub—a centuries-old, mythical institution—is in grave danger. For the first time since the *Domesday Book* was written over a thousand years ago, more than half the villages in the United Kingdom are without pubs. Not so in the United States. The best place to drink an IPA, or a porter for that matter, is no longer London or Burton-on-Trent but more likely Chico or Santa Rosa.

SOBERING TRUTHS

I DO not intend to be falsely naïve or over-idealistic here. It would be dishonest of me to ignore certain sobering truths about beer consumption in the U.S., even though I believe the story I'm telling of Sierra Nevada Brewing Co. is, for the most part, upbeat and optimistic.

The first of these truths is economic. While it is true that Sierra Nevada Brewing Co. continues to reap handsome profits and craft brewers continue to see a growth in overall market share, the fact is, however, that craft brewing sales still account for approximately just 5 percent of the total beer volume consumed in the U.S. Of the 213 million barrels of beer on the U.S. beer market in 2008, the craft brewing industry produced 8.6 million barrels. Yes, it's a significant statistic—but it's still relatively small in scale. As Maureen Ogle observes: "craft brewers may have commandeered a room in the house of brewing, but the rest of the dwelling—the brewing Establishment—remains intact." The fact is that beer drinking habits are still dominated by big breweries with their emphasis on carbonation and sugar over taste and character. This may be changing—but only incrementally. Recently, sales numbers have been flat for "big beer" companies; but they are improving for the craft beer segment. Perhaps consumers are turning away from light beer and craving, instead, a beer with bold flavor and distinction. Perhaps they are beginning to prefer a beer that speaks for itself rather than one that relies on expensive advertising campaigns and cheap gimmicks. We can only hope.

The second consideration is more ominous. The health risks associated with alcohol consumption, particularly the dangers of binge drinking (defined as five or more drinks in a row by most medical authorities) are undisputed. According to the World Health Organization, alcohol abuse is the fifth leading cause of premature death in the world. Of course, beer is not alone in contributing to this alarming statistic. But it is the drink of choice for many, particularly the young. Alcohol abuse, as we know, is a serious public health problem that can cause addiction, cirrhosis of the liver, high blood pressure, fetal alcohol syndrome, and cancer. It can lead to a softening of the brain, with a detrimental impact on mental capacities, particularly for those under the age of twenty-four before their brain is fully developed. Drinking until you are "blind-and-legless" continues to be a rite of initiation in certain quarters. Between 1993 and 2001, there was a spike of 56 percent in the eighteen to twenty-years-old age indulging in group binge-drinking episodes, according to the National Institute on Alcohol Abuse and Alcoholism. Over 1,400 college students die every year in the U.S. as a result of hazardous drinking. This is not to mention the drastic social effects that result from irresponsible drinking: traffic accidents, sexual assaults, increased risk-taking activities, and a possible decline in the quality of academic work.

Locally, the results from a 2007 Chico State survey on alcohol use make for grim reading: 62.8 percent of students reported that they had engaged in binge drinking in the previous two weeks; 52.4 percent reported participating in some form of public misconduct (such as a fight or an altercation with the police) as a result of drinking or drug use. In order to stamp its zero tolerance policy on campus culture, the Chico State administration enacted a range of alcohol control policies from strictly enforcing substance-free halls of residence to staging alcohol-free fairs with the aim of promoting "fun without alcohol."

Well-intentioned as these policies undoubtedly are, I believe that they are fundamentally flawed. Simply saying "no" to alcohol is a message that does not always appeal to young adults. In fact, the message often becomes self-defeating, merely increasing the temptation to taste the forbidden fruit. I believe that it might be more effective to acknowledge that there is a human yearning to experience euphoria and that beer is one of many substances or stimulants that can help to fuel this yearning in young adults. From the Old Testament ("A man hath no better thing under the sun than to drink and to be merry") to the twelfth century Persian poet, Omar Khayyam ("Ah, my Beloved, fill the Cup that clears/ Today of past Regrets and future Fears"), the grape and the grain have consistently been celebrated as vital catalysts of the human spirit.

Like any stimulant, beer is subject to abuse, of course. But rather than deprive our students from it altogether, wouldn't it be better to encourage its mindful enjoyment, to show how the pleasure of drinking beer can be enhanced through sensible, responsible, and moderate practice?

I agree with John Selden, a seventeenth century English essayist, who wrote: "Tis not the drinking that is to be blamed, but the excess." Or, as Charles Bamforth, professor of malting and brewing sciences at University of California, Davis, argues: if we are to appreciate that beer drinking is "part of a respectable, respectful, and restrained lifestyle," then "[T]here is a big education job to be done on beer"—its heritage, traditions, and what he calls its "national provenance" (192–4).

Perhaps a pilot program for this kind of education can be tested here in Chico where the reputation of party school sticks uncomfortably, where we've experienced our share of tragedies from the over-consumption of beer, and where Sierra Nevada

Brewing Co. has a commanding influence. Perhaps we should try to cultivate in consumers a greater awareness about the beer they are drinking—the art and science, craft and care, pride and passion that have gone into its making. Perhaps we could do more to actively discourage the culture of binge drinking that urges an emptying of the mind in order to escape reality; and instead, we would do well to remind ourselves that drinking good beer is an enjoyable way of finding fulfillment and enhancing reality.

HOP(E)S AND DREAMS

THE STORY I have traced in this book is a reminder about the value and importance of fulfilling a dream. Granted, in these days of economic uncertainty, talk of the American dream is often greeted with a measure of justified cynicism. As the comedian George Carlin once quipped, "It's called the American dream because you have to be asleep to believe in it." The bitter truth behind Carlin's words seems particularly apt in the state of California, so long a beacon of hope for the rest of the world yet now beset by crippling budget deficits and a fading collective vision. This is the state, after all, that furnished us with the world's most innovative high-tech companies, the world's largest system of higher education, the world's most famous motion picture industry, the world's most productive breadbasket, not to mention some of the world's most beautiful natural scenery. Nowadays, you're more likely to hear it being described as a basket case, a laughingstock, even a warning to the rest of the world of how not to run an economy. The Golden State, we're told, has a tarnished hue. We seem caught in a web of dysfunctional and depressing news stories.

As a counterpoint, I offer a story that is inspiring, optimistic, and hopeful, a story of innovators and trailblazing entrepreneurs. That they helped to pioneer the craft beer revolution is not only a personal success story; it's also a success story for America, for

California, and for a modest valley town nestled between two
majestic mountain ranges.

Let's raise a glass to salute the promise and power of that enduring dream.

Ken Grossman toasts Sierra Nevada's thirty-year journey

A TIMELINE FOR SIERRA NEVADA BREWING CO.

1,800 B.C. The Sumerian Ode to Ninkasi, goddess of beer, is composed on clay tablets

1621 The German Beer Purity Law declares that only barley, hops, and water (later yeast) are permitted in the making of beer

1849 The California Gold Rush stimulates the popularity of Steam Beer

1857 Louis Pasteur observes that the fermentation of alcohol is caused by living organisms (identified as yeast)

1920–1933 Prohibition lasts thirteen years in the U.S. and decimates the American beer industry

1965 Fritz Maytag purchases Anchor Brewing Company in San Francisco and resurrects Anchor Steam Beer

1969 Fred Eckhardt publishes *A Treatise on Lager Beers*

Summer 1972 Ken Grossman graduates from Taft High School, Woodland Hills, and moves to Chico

1972–1976 Grossman works at various bicycle stores around town

1973 Syndicated columnist, Mike Royko, complains that American beer is "our national shame" and tastes as if "the brewing process involved running it through a horse"

1976 Jack McAuliffe establishes New Albion Brewery in Sonoma, California

1976 Grossman opens The Home Brew Shop in downtown Chico where he meets and befriends Paul Camusi

1978 Charlie Papazian founds the American Homebrewers Association and Association of Brewers

1979 President Jimmy Carter signs into law a bill that legalizes homebrewing

November 15, 1980 Grossman and Camusi brew their first batch (stout) which they pour down their drain because of yeast problems

March 1981 Grossman and Camusi brew their eleventh batch (pale ale) which satisfies them. "Now we could go commercial." They brew five hundred barrels of beer in their first year

1981 Steve Harrison is hired as Sierra Nevada's first employee (responsible for sales and distribution)

1982 Grossman and Camusi tour German breweries and purchase a disused brewhouse from Huppmann in the town of Aschaffenburg

1983 Steve Dresler is hired and later becomes brewmaster

May 1984 An article in the "Sunday Magazine" of *The San Francisco Examiner* offers a rave review of Sierra Nevada Pale Ale

1987 Construction starts of new brewery on 20th Street; installation of Huppmann kettles

November 15, 1988 Brewing commences in 20th Street brewhouse

1989 The Restaurant and Taproom are opened

1993 Production hits six-figures (more than 100,000 barrels a year)

1994 Sierra Nevada goes around the clock (24/7) to keep up with demand

1995–96 The craft brew bubble bursts in the U.S. and is followed by a shakeout of less successful companies

1996 A state-of-the art $2 million bottling line is installed at Sierra Nevada

1997–1998 The West Brewhouse is constructed, increasing production capacity to 800,000 barrels a year

1999 The buyout of Paul Camusi is settled

December 31, 1999 Y2K fears preoccupy the world, as well as Sierra Nevada Brewing Co.

2000 The 350-seat Big Room is opened

2004 The Research and Development Lab is opened alongside the ten-barrel Pilot Brewery

2004 The first season of Sierra Center Stage concerts airs on PBS (from the Big Room)

2005 Four 250-kilowatt fuel cell power units are installed, supplying 1 megawatt of power

2005 Governor Schwarzenegger presents Governor's Environmental and Economic Leadership Award to Ken Grossman

May 2007 Twist-off caps are replaced by pry-off caps on bottles

August 2007 An extensive search and rescue operation is undertaken for Vice President Steve Harrison on the Sacramento River

2008 Beer Camp sessions begin

2007–2010 Notable new beers are added to the Sierra Nevada repertoire, including Harvest, Torpedo, and Kellerweis

2008 An on-site health clinic is opened

2009 The largest privately owned solar array in the U.S. is dedicated, supplying 1.5 megawatts of power

2009 An on-site day care center is opened

November 15, 2010 Sierra Nevada Brewing Co. celebrates its thirtieth anniversary

A PROFILE OF THE BEERS:
THE BREWMASTER, STEVE DRESLER, SPEAKS

IN APRIL 2009, I sat down with Steve Dresler, Sierra Nevada's long-serving brewmaster, to discuss the history behind the company's best-known beers. Here's a transcript of the interview.

Pale Ale

When I started in 1983, this was our core beer and still remains our flagship beer to this day. It was, originally, very much a fringe beer: a 38 BU (bitterness unit) beer with a relatively high alcohol at 5.6 percent. But, most uniquely of all, it was bottle conditioned. I know that, even to some of the people who were giving Ken advice at the time, like Dr. Michael Lewis from UC Davis, this was a whacky thought. Not only was it a bitter beer but it also had a huge aroma which was simply not common in the mainstream drinking circles.

When I came on board in 1983, we weren't doing filtration so we were using traditional finings, and therefore the beers had a heavier yeast load. We started filtering in 1984 and cleaned the flavor up a bit.

But the beer recipe is still basically identical, heavily featuring Cascade hops (being the first U.S.-bred aroma hop). The only thing we've changed over time is our use of some of the associated hops, the bittering hops. But the malt body is the same and the Cascade aroma is the same.

In my opinion, it's the best beer out there! It's my core beer at home, and it's my wife's favorite beer.

Crystal Wheat

This is one of my favorite beers. I like the lightness of it and its aroma. Basically, the way this fell together is that Ken and I were doing hop selection in Yakima one September. We're always interested in what's new and available. So we were presented with a new hop variety called Crystal. Very nice aroma. Lemon-grass, citrus, a little bit of spice. We decided to buy some. For whatever reason—the aroma of the hop, or the crisp character of the malt flavor—something just clicked in my brain. We came back to Chico and put one together. It's a beer that has become very popular here in the pub. It's got a big perception yet it's a small, lower alcohol beer. Perfect for a hot day or a midday meal here at the brewery.

Porter and Stout

Ken started out with darker ales. Stout was his first batch. Sometimes, the darker ales are more forgiving because they don't have the finer flavor nuances of, say, the Pale Ale. The Stout and the Porter have changed quite a bit more over the years than the Pale Ale. We've reworked them recently and I really like the way they are now. We've taken the Stout and spun it more towards the original ingredient list. We've gone back to a similar grist composition and to the original hop varieties that we were using in the 1980s. It's a drier stout now than it used to be.

The Porter, on the other hand, we're moving away from the Stout by lightening up the color a little bit, dropping the bitterness down as well as the hop aroma. With dark ales, you can really get into a conflicting battle between hops and malt. We're big hop people here and one of our tendencies has been sometimes to over-hop our beers. So you might get a black malt that tastes too bitter. The beer becomes too astringent. With the Porter, I'm really trying to get more of the coffee, chocolate note and not have the astringency that sometimes comes in combination with the hop.

With the Stout, we're trying to bring in a drier, darker character, lessen the hops, and increase the drinkability.

Celebration

Celebration had just started when I came to the brewery in 1983. I remember Ken was incredibly proud because in his hop selection that year—he had gotten some phenomenally beautiful Cascades that had come off some young plants. The aromatics were incredible. I assume that's what got him into making this holiday beer.

The Celebration Ale really fits the mould of big-hopped IPAs (India pale ales). It has become our seasonal cornerstone. It's a huge product for us. It's got everything: a beautiful look, a beautiful aroma, a wonderful package, a great history. It's anticipated by everybody. The beauty of that beer is that we only brew it right after the hop harvest. So it's freshly hopped for the best aroma. If we select the hops on September 5, then we're brewing on September 7. I go up to Yakima every year for this annual ritual. We prioritize Cascade, Centennial, and Chinook hop varieties. Then the dry-hopping gives it the other bump in its aromatic quality. It is truly a beautiful, beautiful beer. In my opinion, if you want an IPA that gives you everything—hop bitterness, aroma, warming alcohol—in one package, it's Celebration Ale.

Bigfoot

The barley wine here is a craft American spin on traditional ales. It's hoppy as hell with big, big bitterness. Yet it's also a malty beer. It runs 95 bitterness units. For some, it's a confusing beer because it's a barley wine but, oh my god, what's this aroma?

In 1983–4, it immediately became a cult beer. There are probably more stories rotating around Bigfoot—and the evils of Bigfoot—than any other. Bigfoot drinkers are passionate about their Bigfoot. It has a totally different effect on an individual. It's an incredibly labor-intensive, difficult beer to make. But it's a beer that people look forward to every season.

People are beginning to do vertical tastings of barley wine over the years. Of all the beers, it ages the best. A three-year-old or five-year-old barley wine can be phenomenally good.

Flavors change totally over the years. Certain flavors go away; other flavors come to the forefront. After five years, for example, the brashness and hoppiness go away; the mellowness and maltiness, the wood and the molasses come through. It's a totally different beer. It's lovely!

Torpedo

This beer came out of Ken's creative thinking. He asked: *How do you get a dry-hopped quality in a beer when you don't have enough tanks to dry hop?* So Ken had this idea to take the beer out of the tank, circulate it through an external tank of hops, then bring it back into the original tank, as opposed to taking a tank of beer and moving it into another tank of beer with the hops in it. In order to dry-hop the beer, ordinarily, I need two tanks. But with Torpedo, you need just one tank, just a single fermenter. So this allowed me to greatly increase my production, and come up with some markedly different beers, and not have to greatly expand my infrastructure. The extraction of the hops is much more efficient. The quality of the aroma in the Torpedo Ale is great. We finally had the technology and innovation in place to make the IPA that we really wanted to do.

We call it Torpedo because we're shooting the beer through the hops. The beer is phenomenal. We did a wonderful blend of Magnum hops (which have a great aroma and high oil percentage) augmented with the Crystal hop (which has got a citrus, lemony spin to it). Then we discovered a brand new variety of hop called Citra; we added just a pinch of that to the Torpedo. Citra has a unique, tropical fruit citrus aroma combo. Used lightly, it can be very delicate. So we constructed layers of flavor, aroma, and complexity. You don't pin anything down. The aromas just play off each other. The Torpedo is very complicated. I'm really proud of it. It's unique to Sierra Nevada. Most breweries would not need to use this technology because they use a hop-pellet product. But because we hold to the basic belief that true aroma and taste only come from whole-cone hops, then you go to these lengths without taking shortcuts.

Anniversary

We've done Anniversary for two years now. It's a season-al, brewed in the summer, right before Celebration Ale. I look around to see what I have to brew with (because I'm not at the point of harvest procurement yet), and we're trying to produce something that celebrates the history of our brewery. Immediate-ly, I think of King Cascades, going back to the roots of our brew-ery: let's make a lighter IPA, what I refer to as a "session IPA" that really features where we came from. It's a torpedoed beer. We do use the secondary hop technique on it. So I figured, let's take Pale Ale, bring it up into the lower end of the IPA category, and then do the post-fermentation hopping technique on it, which really brings out the aroma. It's a wonderful beer. When you're drink-ing beer, 90 percent of your sensory perception is in the nose, so you've got the perception of a big beer but it's a session beer, very drinkable, very worker-friendly.

Hefeweizen

This is a really interesting transition for us. We came out with a bottled wheat beer about eleven or twelve years ago, an Ameri-can style wheat beer. Other breweries were doing the same, call-ing their beer a Hefeweizen but they weren't. Hefeweizens are specific to strains of yeast that give them traditional, Germanic flavor profiles. Since we didn't call ours a Hefeweizen, the beer never really took off.

A few years ago, we started on a beer called "Ruthless," named after Ruth Martin, one of our lab supervisors. She did all the yeast work and propagation for us on this. We started playing around with true Hefeweizen yeast strains. The beer was never quite right. Ken loves Hefeweizen. So he and I went over to Germany last November with Scott Jennings from the Pilot Lab. So we pulled up in Nuremburg and started a tour through Bavaria of different Hefeweizen breweries for five days, learning what these people were doing, and drinking beers which were exquisite. They were very open with information. We toured through their fermentation rooms, learned how they handled their yeast. Yeast management had been one of our critical flaws. We learned a ton. We came back and put what we learned to play, using the same strain. All the things started clicking. All of a sudden, we were getting very consistent banana, clove aromatics in the beer which is what you want.

A lot of women in our sensory group say that Hefeweizen will attract women drinkers to the bars. They don't want 7 percent alcohol, big hoppy beers. What they get with Hefeweizen is around 5 percent alcohol yet very flavorful. It's a nice breakaway from our main family of beers. It's not hop-based. It's a yeast-based beer with very little bitterness to it. All the flavor, complexity, and aroma come from the yeast. It's a totally different challenge for us.

THE BREWERY TOUR

I F YOU want a Willy Wonka experience of Sierra Nevada's brewing operation, don't miss the opportunity for a guided tour. Start in the Gift Shop area where you will be greeted by Marie Gray, tour guide coordinator, or one of her assistants. After hearing a brief historical overview of the brewery, you will then be guided through seven key staging areas in the brewery.

Here's what you'll see on the guided tour:

(1) **The Mill Room.** This is where the barley malt is ground and mixed with hot water to create a cereal mash or wort. The room consists of a grain mill and mash tun.

(2) **The West Brewhouse.** This is the heart and soul of the brewery. The room consists of two beautiful copper brew kettles that were hammered into shape by retired German coppersmiths in 1997 (and deliberately fashioned to resemble Sierra Nevada's original Huppmann kettles located in the East Brewhouse, which you can see as you enter the Taproom and Restaurant on your right, through the glass window). The room also contains a lauter tun and whirlpool vessel.

Notice the wall murals that celebrate the sequential steps of the brewing process in a style reminiscent of the popular American artist, Thomas Hart Benton.

(3) **The Hop Freezer.** Take a deep breath before you enter the hop storage room: not just because the room is deliberately kept at near freezing temperatures (to preserve the freshness of the whole cone hops), but also because hop aromas fill the room (and most likely, your nose). To get a full sensory experience, plunge your hand into a bin of hops, gently rub the flowers together with your fingers, and inhale deeply. Don't worry, it's legal.

(4) **The Quality Assurance Lab.** As you walk along the hall-

way from the hop freezer to the Quality Assurance Lab, notice the illustrated ceramic tiles along the wall: each one is handcrafted and depicts a different scene related to the history and culture of beer.

Quality and consistency are two of the most important guiding principles at Sierra Nevada, and this lab is where the principles are researched and applied with the help of cutting-edge technology.

(5) **The 800-Room Cellar.** After yeast is pitched into the wort, fermentation takes place in these 800-barrel closed tanks. (Sierra Nevada also has four 100-barrel open square fermenters which are not included in the tour, but can be seen through the window at the kitchen-end of the bar in the Taproom).

(6) **The Rooftop Catwalk.** In order to get from the cellar to the bottling line, you'll take a footway that offers an impressive view of Sierra Nevada's energy workhorses: the four hydrogen fuel cells on your right, and the extensive solar array that covers almost every available rooftop all around you.

(7) **The Packaging and Racking Area.** Before entering the packaging and racking area, you'll need to don safety glasses and insert earplugs. The noise level is intense when thousands of bottles are shunted along fast-moving assembly lines. This bottling line is capable of packaging fifty-six cases of beer a minute! In the adjoining racking room, close to 300 full-sized kegs and roughly 330 five-gallon kegs are filled every hour. It's easy to be hypnotized by the frantic yet carefully controlled energy of this space.

At the end of your tour, you'll hopefully have an increased respect and appreciation for the Sierra Nevada beer that arrives daily on your dinner table.

Aguided tour typically lasts for just over an hour. In case you're pressed for time, or you're not able to take a tour, you can also check out some of the same staging areas at your own pace from strategically placed viewing windows. Start in the Gift Shop area, then climb a flights of stairs to the Big Room lobby (be sure to check out the hop motifs carefully engraved on the granite stairs).

Here's what you'll see on your self tour:

(1) **The Big Room Lobby.** This is where you'll find ancient artifacts from Sierra Nevada's original brewery on Gilman Way, together with miscellaneous contraptions acquired along the way: filtration machines, various wood instruments (such as malting paddles), beer taps, hydrometers, beer mugs, cleaning brushes, an ancient bottling machine that looks like a Dalek from the *Doctor Who* television series, several racking machines (that should not be mistaken for medieval torture instruments), and bottles of original Sierra Nevada brews as well as other breweries (in display cabinets against the walls). There's also a video that you can watch, showcasing the history of the brewery; it's divided into five short chapters, each ten to fifteen minutes long: Overview, History, Ingredients, Brewing and Filtration, Bottling and Racking.

To further stimulate the senses, be sure to smell the mason jars of malt and whole-cone hops.

(2) **First Observation Window.** You'll notice the grain mill and mash tun where the barley malt is ground and mashed into cereal wort.

(3) **Viewing Gallery of the West Brewhouse.** Here you'll have a bird's eye view of the beautiful copper brew kettles, lauter tun, and whirlpool vessel.

(4) **Lobby Observation Window.** After returning to the lobby, check out the view of closed fermentation tanks through

the window on the far side of the room.

Afterwards, be sure to adjourn to the Taproom and sample the finished product!

INTERVIEW WITH HEAD CHEF MICHEAL ILES

Savoring the Big Fat Mouth

ICHEAL IS Sierra Nevada's head chef and an Elvis Costello look-alike. When I ask him to explain the increasing popularity of beer-food pairings, he cites various reasons. The most obvious is the price of quality beer as opposed to quality wine. He also points out that the wide variety of flavors in beer lends itself to innovation and experimentation, and this can be exciting for a chef. He goes on to use words like "enhance," "contrast," and "balance" when it comes to matching the flavors of different beers with food styles from around the world. The other favorite words in his cooking lexicon are "depth" and "accent." What he's looking for when he cooks, he tells me, are "flavors that cover the whole tongue."

What follows is a transcription of a short interview I conducted with him, pairing Sierra Nevada beers with his favorite foods—in an attempt to find the perfect formula for creating what he likes to call "a big fat mouth."

Pale Ale

 Pale Ale has a complex character with heavy use of Cascade hops. It's an aggressive beer. We're from California; this is a California beer, so I love pairing this beer with Mexican food. I think it's fabulous with all that cilantro and spicy flavors. It's also good with beef. But the perfect match is with spicy Mexican food.

Recommendation: Pork carnitas, roast tomatillo, and malt salsa

IPA and Torpedo Extra IPA

The IPA was invented on those long shipping hauls to India. It has even more aggressive hop flavors than the Pale Ale. I love Indian and Thai food with it, especially Thai food that has creaminess from the coconut which can balance out and flatten out the beer. Hot chilies enable your tongue to absorb the nuances of the flavors that are in the Torpedo. If you sit down with a plate of our Thai seafood curry and drink IPA with it, you'll absolutely love it! You'll go, "Wow! I didn't realize this beer was so palatable."

Recommendation: Thai seafood curry with spice rubbed slow roasted portabella mushrooms

Porter

The name comes from the East End laborers (of London) who carried goods from the docks to the warehouse. It's a heavily malted beer, dark, and wonderful with desserts. I love Porter with cake and cinnamon, ginger, nutmeg. Historically, it fits—because these are the spices the porters were carrying from the docks. Plum pudding is wonderful with Porter. I also like vanilla ice cream with a little shot glass of Porter. When you match them, you get wonderful flavors which you would not get just by the drinking the beer by itself.

Recommendation: Plum pudding

Bigfoot

This is an extremely difficult beet to pair with food. Maybe a stilton or blue cheese might be able to stand up to it. Possible even cigars! That's a big, fat sipping beer.

Recommendation: Blue cheese and stuffed medjool dates

Stout

Stout is very dark and rich with lots of roasted flavors. So for me, I love smoked fish with stout and I also love chocolate with it. Irish stew goes well, of course, especially when it's made with lamb because of its rich, gamey flavor.

Recommendation: Stout cake

Celebration Ale

A time-honored, wonderful beer. Lots of malt, lots of hops. It's dry-hopped and delicate. It's only available for a short period of time. Right now (November), we're serving it with different salamis and medium-firm cheeses like Gouda. It's a big beer that also goes well with spicy sausages.

Recommendation: Blood sausage and blue cheeses

Summerfest

This is a beautiful beer with all kinds of seafood, especially scallops and prawns. Even spicy Mexican food goes down well.

Recommendation: Sautéed garlic shrimp

Harvest Ale

Because it's a big, fat beer, it's great with grilled salmon, tandoori chicken or roasted tomatoes. The hops are fresh and the beer is very grassy, so basil works well with it and balances the flavors out nicely. Goat cheese is also good.

Recommendation: Tandoori chicken and roasted tomatoes

Kellerweis

An amazing beer with heavy yeast presence that tastes like bananas. We're using it a lot with Thai food because of the bananas and the caramel. It's also good with soft cheeses like brie. It's a rich, deep beer so we did some scallop dishes with it which worked out great. It's also nice with stewed tomatoes and bouillabaisse.

Recommendation: Grilled mahi and chili salsa

Southern Hemisphere Harvest Ale

It's a little more "oomphish" with more hop and bitter flavors. We did couscous with chicken and Moroccan spices. Cracked crab also works well. So do whole-grain pastas. I try to balance out all that "oomph" and flavor.

Recommendation: Roasted lemon chicken and couscous

"What about fish and chips?" I ask at the end of our beer roundup.

"Oh, of course," he apologizes. "I sell more fish and chips than any other item on the menu. That's probably why I overlooked it. We're still using the same recipe as twenty years ago, except now I add Kellerweis to the batter instead of Crystal Wheat. The beauty of fish and chips is that they go with any beer you like. Just take your pick."

BEER AND BIKES

GIVEN THE Grossman family's long-standing association with cycling as a sport (eldest brother, Steve, raced in Europe in the late '70s and early '80s; Ken and son, Brian, both raced competitively) and the brewery's involvement with the local cycling club, Chico Velo, it's only natural that the brewery should sponsor its own professional bike team. In 2003 it cosponsored the Sierra Nevada/Clif Bar professional cycling team, solely sponsored the Sierra Nevada pro team in 2004, and cosponsored a team with Kodak Gallery from 2005 to 2007. The team sported yellow and gold lycra jerseys and raced at several international events. It was the first professional sports team in the U.S. to go carbon neutral—purchasing energy credits and offsets, using hybrid vehicles for transportation to events, and cutting down on unnecessary energy usage. Despite the termination of professional cycling in 2008, the brewery has continued to support amateur bike teams and to sponsor regional and local cycling events such as the Tour of California and Chico's Wild-flower Century.

The 2006 Kodak Gallery / Sierra Nevada Professional Cycling Team. Left to right, back: Eric Chu (mechanic), Jonas Carney (sports director), Kurt Stockton (owner, operations manager), Dominique Perras, Martin Gilbert, Dan Schmatz, David Robinson, Ben Jacques-Maynes, Jason Allen, Jesse Anthony, Pete Lopinto, Robin Zellner (owner, race manager), Josh Kadis (marketing manager), Joanne Fusco (soigneur). Left to right, front: Scott Zwizanski, Mike Dietrich, Jackson Stewart, Skyler Bishop. Courtesy Kodak Gallery / Sierra Nevada professional cycling team and Kurt Stockton.

THE BIRTH OF A DREAM: AN EXTRACT FROM SIERRA NEVADA'S 1979 BUSINESS PLAN

How the Beer Is Made and How the Brewery Will Function

The basic process is the same for large and small breweries. The principal grain cereal is barley. It grows almost everywhere, from the plateaus of Tibet to the Egyptian Sahara Oasis, even inside the Arctic Circle, but there is none finer than the barley grown on the great flat plains of America. And that is where we will get ours. Barley is readied for brewing by a natural process called malting. Malt is grain that has undergone careful steeping, germinating and kiln-drying procedures.

Hops, the second ingredient, are the blossoms of beautiful vines, grown in Europe and America. They are very important as they add seasoning and aroma, the individual character of each type of beer.

The brewers yeast will be our own select strain of isolated cloned cells that work the fermentation, by acting on the malt sugars and extracted hop juices as it brews in tubs of well water. From this concoction, called wort, the miracle of "liquid bread" begins. Nothing else is added.

After this initial fermentation, the beer is aged to mellowness. Uncle Sam meters the brew for his taxes before the bottling, then the product is packaged and sent to the consumer.

All along the way, every brewer can opt for variations in quality, process, taste and flavor, age and color. His choices are his secret formulas, his pedigreed yeasts, the key to his kingdom.

The results, as in cooking a fine dish, are only as good as the basic ingredients and the talents that blend them.

Ingredients in Our Beer:

No Chemical Additives: We are all concerned about the number and variety of chemicals added to extend, preserve and fortify the food and drink we consume. Commercial beers can contain up to fifty-nine artificial additives. Many are actually harmful chemicals. We're so used to tasting them we do not realize how delicious and smooth beer can be without them. Our beer is one hundred percent fresh and pure as good beer used to be.

Barley: Our barley malt will come from San Francisco and Canada. We will be using nothing but malt. All large brewers add rice or corn to obtain a cheaper extract. This is the prime reason for the poor, thin taste of American beers.

Hops: We will use the finest American hops, grown in Washington and Oregon. Many brewers use pulverized hops that are turned into pellets or extracts of the hop resins. We will use only whole fresh hops.

Yeast: The billions of yeast cells present in each fermentation will be cultured from a single cell which was originally bred to possess the finest brewing characteristics. Yeast is the secret ingredient in our beer. Our laboratory experience helps insure us of a superior beer.

Water: One of the prime reasons for locating in this area is the excellent quality of the water. Chico has one of the best city water systems in California. Our brewing water will be brought up from deep wells 500–1,000 feet. This location solves elaborate filtering problems for us and helps insure a quality tasting beer.

Natural Carbonation: Like good champagne, the best beers develop their carbonation in the bottle naturally. They are not pumped full of carbon dioxide as are so many commercial beers. The head is creamy and full. It consists of super-fine bubbles that only result from natural fermentation in the bottle.

GLOSSARY OF TERMS

adjuncts   Starches such as corn, sugar, and rice used predominantly by big beer companies (but frowned upon by craft brewing companies) to replace or supplement the traditional ingredients in beer.

alcohol by volume (a.b.v.)   A measure of the amount of alcohol in a beer.

ale   A style of beer, often hearty and robust, made with top fermenting yeast and brewed at temperatures between 60 and 70 degrees Fahrenheit.

attenuation   The degree to which yeast consumes fermentable sugars, converting them into alcohol and carbon dioxide, usually expressed as a percentage amount.

barley   The grain used to produce malt in beer; craft brewers prefer to use high-quality two-row barley (so named because of the number of rows of kernels on a stalk) whereas big beer companies find the six-row varieties are better suited for mashing adjuncts such as corn and rice.

barrel   A commonly used unit of measurement to describe volume of beer production. One barrel equals approximately thirty-one gallons or two kegs or about sixty 6-packs.

big beer   A phrase often used to refer to the industrial-sized, multinational breweries such as Anheuser-Busch InBev and MillerCoors, in contrast with the fifteen hundred craft breweries around the U.S.

bitterness units (I.B.U)   An international counting system for measuring the hop bitterness in a beer.

bottle conditioning   A process of secondary fermentation whereby small amounts of yeast are added to the beer during the bottling stage, thus allowing for natural carbonation and complex flavors.

brew kettles   The vessels used for boiling the wort mixed with hops, for up to two hours. Often they are the central showpiece of a craft brewery because of their sleek copper exterior.

brewpub   An establishment that brews and sells its own beer on the premises.

cask conditioning   Similar to bottle conditioning, except the yeast is added to the cask (or firkin) rather than the bottle. Because of the natural carbonation produced during secondary fermentation, the beer is often served from the cask without need of further carbon dioxide pressure.

craft brewery   A brewery that uses traditional brewing methods and traditional brewing ingredients (malt, hops, yeast, and water) to brew from 15,000 to 2 million barrels of beer a year.

distribution   The system whereby beer is shipped and marketed by wholesalers to retailers for resale to consumers.

dry-hopping   The addition of dry hops to the wort after it has cooled, thereby adding a special hop character to the finished product.

fermentation   The process whereby yeast converts the sugars in the wort into alcohol and carbon dioxide.

filtration   The process whereby sediments and residual yeast are removed in order to render the beer stable.

flocculation   The answer to all of life's burning question. Alternatively stated, it refers to the clumping of yeast particles together after they have consumed the sugars in the wort: top-fermenting ale yeasts flocculate to form a crust on the surface of the beer whereas bottom-fermenting lager yeasts flocculate to the bottom to create a layer of sediment.

homebrewing   The brewing of an alcoholic beverage (predominantly beer) on a small scale, usually at home for noncommercial reasons. As a carryover from Prohibition, homebrewing was illegal in the U.S. until 1979 when it was legalized by federal law. However, because states have the right to ignore this particular federal ruling, homebrewing is still illegal in some states such as Alabama and Mississippi.

hops   The flowers from a vine that impart bitterness, flavor, and aroma to beer.

lager: A style of beer, often crisp and clean, made with bottom-fermenting yeast and brewed at temperatures between 40 and 50 degrees Fahrenheit and stored at cooler temperatures than ale.

lauter tun   The brewing vessel that separates the mash (spent malt grains) from the liquid wort.

mash tun   The vessel used early on in the brewing process to create the mash by soaking malt grains in hot water, thereby converting the starches from the malt into fermentable sugars.

microbrewery   The term used often in the late '70s and 1980s to describe small, startup breweries. In the mid-1980s, the term craft brewery began to be used more often in its place. Technically, a microbrewery and craft brewery share similar philosophical approaches to the art and science of beer making—the major difference being production capacity (any figure less than 15,000 barrels now qualifies as a microbrewery).

oxidation   Oxygen is a brewer's best friend and worst enemy, as Ken Grossman discovered early on in his beer-making efforts. While aeration is good for beer in the initial stages of production, the introduction of oxygen (oxidation) after fermentation can cause serious problems to the taste and texture of beer.

Reinheitsgebot   Sometimes known as the German Beer Purity Law of 1516, it declared that only barley, hops, and water were the only ingredients allowed in the production of beer (later, yeast was added to the list).

wort   Liquid malt or unfermented beer.

yeast   The tiny single-celled organisms responsible for magically transforming fermentable sugars into alcohol. Even though there are hundreds of varieties and strains, yeasts are usually classified into two major categories: top-fermenting (for making ale) and bottom-fermenting (for making lager).

WORKS CITED

Bakan, Joel. *The Corporation: The Pathological Pursuit of Profit and Power.* New York, Free Press, 2004.

Bamforth, Charles. *Grape vs. Grain: A Historical, Technological, and Social Comparison of Wine and Beer.* New York, Cambridge University Press, 2008.

Baum, Dan. *Citizen Coors: An American Dynasty.* New York: William Morrow, 200.

Burch, Byron. *Quality Brewing: A Guidebook for the Home Production of Fine Beers.* Richmond: Joby, 1974.

Calagione, Sam. *Brewing Up a Business: Adventures in Entrepreneurship from the founder of Dogfish Head.* New Jersey: Wiley, 2005.

————. "Extreme Brewing in America." *Beer and Philosophy: The Unexamined Beer Isn't Worth Drinking.* Ed. Steven Hales. Oxford: Blackwell, 2007.

Castleman, Michael. "The Beer That's Making Chico Famous." *San Francisco Examiner: Image Magazine.* 25 May, 1986: 23–27.

Cornell, Martyn. *Beer: The Story of the Pint.* London: Headline, 2003.

Eckhardt, Fred. *A Treatise on Lager Beers: An Anthology of American and Canadian Lager Beer.* Portland: Hobby Winemaker, 1970.

Hales, Steven, ed. *Beer and Philosophy: The Unexamined Beer Isn't Worth Drinking.* Oxford: Blackwell, 2007.

Hawken, Paul. *Blessed Unrest: How the Largest Movement in the World Came into Being and Why No One Saw It Coming.* New York: Viking, 2007.

Hindy, Steve, and Tom Potter. *Beer School: Bottling Success at the Brooklyn Brewery.* New Jersey: Wiley, 2005.

Jackson, Michael. *Beer Companion: The World's Greatest Beer Styles, Gastronomy, and Traditions.* Philadelphia: Running Press, 1993.

Kingsolver, Barbara. *Animal, Vegetable, Miracle: A Year of Food Life.* New York: HarperCollins, 2007.

Krebs, Peter. *Redhook: Beer Pioneer.* New York: Four Walls Eight Windows, 1998.

Lewis, Michael, and Tom Young. *Brewing.* New York: Aspen, 2001.

McDonough, William, and Michael Braungart. *Cradle to Cradle: Remaking the Way We Make Things.* New York: North Point, 2002.

Noon, Mark. *Yuengling: A History of America's Oldest Brewery.* Jefferson: McFarland, 2005.

Ogle, Maureen. *Ambitious Brew: The Story of American Beer.* New York: Harcourt, 2006.

Papazian, Charlie. *Microbrewed Adventures: A Lupulin-Filled Journey to the Heart and Flavor of the World's Great Craft Beers.* New York: HarperCollins, 2005.

Royko, Mike. *Slats Grobnik and Some Other Friends.* New York: Popular Library, 1976.

Savitz, Andrew. *The Triple Bottom Line: How Today's Best-Run Companies Are Achieving Economic, Social, and Environmental Success—And How You Can Too.* San Francisco: Jossey-Bass, 2006.

Yaeger, Brian. "Kids in the Brewhouse: Second Generation Brewers." *All About Beer.* May 2009: 22-28, 81.

———. *Red, White, and Brew: An American Beer Odyssey.* New York: St. Martin's Griffin, 2008.

INDEX

business vision   143, 155,
    160, 161, 178
co-writes Draught Beer Quality
    Manual   137
craft brewing pioneer   27,
    141
first batch of homemade
    beer   45
first visits Chico   40
mechanical skills   47, 48, 53,
    54, 58, 61, 97
opens The Home Brew
    Shop   55
respects competitors   178
sole owner and CEO   108
sustainable lifestyle   121
teenager   44, 47
Grossman, Sierra   57, 72, 130,
    137
Grossman, Steve   44, 58, 135,
    202
group health plan   155
Guinness   25, 91, 147
Guttmann Brauerei   133
Guy, Eleanor   46, 136

H

Harrison, Steve   79, 89
Harvey, Chuck   61
Harvey, Jean   61
Hathor   29
Hawken, Paul   149
Heineken   76, 106, 147
Hendrix, Jimi   115
Hofmeier, Richard   133
Hoiland, Ed   95

homebrewing   13, 14, 21, 32,
    35, 45, 46, 54, 55, 175
  legalized in 1979   35, 175
The Home Brew Shop   55, 57
hop harmony   112, 149, 167
hops
  Cascade   65, 76, 88, 131
  Centennial   131
  Cluster   76
  Fuggles   16
  Goldings   16
  Motueka   131
  on-site hop field   125, 158,
    162
  Pacific Hallertau   131
  Southern Cross   131
Hudson Valley Brewery   32
Hummer, David   18
Hungerford, John   47
Huppmann brewing vessels   82
  installing   97
  transporting   83

I

InBev   15
Institute of Brewing   23
International Brewers Guild   23

J

Jackson, Michael   20, 21, 55,
    150
Jamaican Dragon Stout   145
John Bidwell   37
John Harvard's Brew House   32
Johnson, Hal   164
Joplin, Laura   110

ABOUT THE AUTHOR

Rob Burton was born and raised in England. Since 1988, he has been professor of English at California State University, Chico. He is the author of *Around the World in 52 Words: Ritual Writing for the New Millennium* (2002) and *Artists of the Floating World: Contemporary Writers Between Cultures* (2007).